Hiking Great Smoky Mountains

Fourth Edition

D0967266

Rodney and Priscilla Albright

revised and edited by
Doris Gove

The
Globe
Pequot
Press

Guilford, Connecticut

Photograph on page viii by Rodney Albright. Remaining photographs appear courtesy of Great Smoky Mountains National Park.

Library of Congress Cataloging-in-Publication Data

Albright, Rodney.
   Hiking Great Smoky Mountains / by Rodney and Priscilla Albright; revised and edited by Doris Gove. — 4th ed.
        p.   cm.
    ISBN 0-7627-0224-9
    1. Hiking—Great Smoky Mountains National Park (N.C. and Tenn.)—Guidebooks. 2. Trails—Great Smoky Mountains National Park (N.C. and Tenn.)—Guidebooks. 3. Great Smoky Mountains National Park (N.C. and Tenn.)—Guidebooks. I. Albright, Priscilla. II. Gove, Doris. III. Title.
GV199.42.G73A4 1999
917.68'8904'53—dc21

98-37831
CIP

♻ This book is printed on recycled paper.
Manufactured in the United States of America
Fourth Edition/Second Printing

Contents

List of Maps

These trail maps are accurate simplifications. Contours have been reduced to 500-foot intervals, the scale kept as large in each instance as possible, to show as much of the overall terrain as is feasible on the small page. On all maps, north is at the top of the page—with one exception, Hazel Creek (Walk 35), where it is indicated on the side. For ease of identification, each map depicts its featured trail or trails with a black dotted line.

Acknowledgments

We readily acknowledge that this guide represents far more than our own efforts. Every person we talked to in the National Park Service was friendly, patient in listening to our questions, and constructive in response. The rangers provided the information on where to walk, and the naturalists were always able to help us identify birds, plants, or trees about which we had questions. Many of these people are not known to us by name. We do appreciate the overall help and guidance provided by Stanley G. Canter and the time spent by Ed Easton in reviewing the original manuscript.

A special thanks goes to Dick Zani, who read our draft manuscript carefully and provided us with much detailed information in regard to trail markings, access roads, and other technicalities. In addition he went out of his way to be helpful and encouraging and to brief us carefully in the matters of park policy and philosophy.

Our thanks to Sally McMillan and Kathylee Baigas, whose honest criticism has been most constructive and who have edited the text scrupulously, and to Connie McLeod, who struggled through all to type the final manuscript.

Grateful acknowledgment is extended to Leroy Fox of Knoxville, Tennessee, and William A. Hart, Jr., of Arden, North Carolina, for assistance and advice on various items.

Thanks also to members of the Smoky Mountains Hiking Club for information and good companionship on hikes for the fourth edition.

The Road Less Traveled

Introduction

The elements have pummelled the slopes of the Great Smoky Mountains for hundreds of millions of years. Once they stood higher than the much younger Rocky Mountains of Colorado. But the ceaseless pounding of storms, the deterioration caused by extremes of temperatures, and the slow, constant pressures of exposure have worn them smooth, mellowed them, and given them their very distinctive character.

Despite the Smokies' southerly location, the Ice Age left its mark by pushing large numbers of rare botanical specimens into the coves. Today a great variety of hardwood trees, flowering plants and shrubs, ferns, mosses, lichens, and mushrooms form a comfortable blanket over the old mountains and play host to a large assemblage of birds and other wild creatures. The Smokies are beautiful, enchanting, mysterious, and grand.

The oval-shaped parcel of 800 square miles that makes up Great Smoky Mountains National Park is crossed by a highway, the Newfound Gap Road, in only one place. From this highway, the Foothills Parkway, or the Blue Ridge Parkway, it is possible to look out over magnificent vistas, to count hazy crests, to see dainty wisps of fog lying in dark, secluded coves, and to say that you have seen the Smokies. But if you are going to feel the majesty of these great mountains, you must walk in them.

The area is crisscrossed by close to 900 miles of trails, and the Park Service maintains as many as they can each year. Most are old footpaths, bridle trails, and logging or fire roads, and there are even ancient Indian paths. If you have an urge to hear the forest murmurs, to smell the mingled fragrances of damp coves, and to taste the sweetness of a mountain morning, it will require a little effort—but it is worth it. Get out on some of these trails. It is the only way.

This guide describes many of the trails in the park you can get

1

to from a road. Any of them is worth taking. You will have some climbing to do, but don't try to make an endurance contest out of your effort. Set your own pace to enjoy yourself. Stop often to rest, look around, and take in what you see.

Our notion of a walk is that it will take you four or five hours and that you will carry a simple lunch to enjoy in a leisurely fashion along the way. In each of the walks we have described, we give an objective and clues to what to expect. We have labeled them easy, moderate, or strenuous to indicate increasing degrees of effort required. Don't be intimidated by these designations. Most of these trails go on for miles, so you can make any one easier by turning back sooner. And, remember, you can walk on farther if you wish. When returning, you can usually look forward to seeing something quite different from what you saw on the way in. Just the subtle change in light puts everything in a different perspective, and you will notice things that were invisible before.

A number of significant changes have occurred in the atmosphere and in the forests of the higher peaks of the Smokies since this book was originally written. First, the blue mist that gave the mountains the name of Smoky—a result of the exhalation of vapor through the leaves of the forest—is now more of a gray cloud formed from a variety of chemical pollutants. Nitrous oxides, sulfur dioxides, and hydrocarbons from auto and industrial pollution have altered considerably the once clean air of the high Smokies. The best time for clear views is after a drenching rain has temporarily removed the offending chemicals.

The second change is in the Fraser fir and red spruce forests at an elevation above 5,000 feet. The once closed canopy of these forests has been opened by the destruction wrought by the balsam woolly adelgid, a sap-sucking insect that kills the mature Fraser fir trees. The Park Service has been unable to control the damage caused by this tiny insect but continues to study the few healthy firs left in hopes of finding more resistant trees. For now, these high woodlands are woven with gray tree skeletons, blackberry vines, shrubs, and thickets of seedling and sapling firs that have sprouted in the sunlight of the opened canopy. Red spruce has been slowed in growth by pollution but still affords greenery in these once magnificent forests.

Third is the reintroduction of the river otter and the red wolf to this area. In 1986 eleven river otters were released in Abrams Creek, which runs from Cades Cove to Chilhowee Lake. The project has been successful, and the otters have slowly increased to the point where a lucky fisherman occasionally chances upon one.

The red wolf was reintroduced in the Cades Cove area in 1991 with two adults and two cubs. A few more wolves were freed in 1993, as part of an effort to control the population of the European wild boar, a non-native animal that damages the soil, muddies creeks and springs, and feeds on wildflower bulbs. As of 1998, the success of wolf reintroduction remains uncertain. (Studies are also underway on the possibility of elk reintroduction.)

Fourth is the continuation of the Adopt-a-Trail project. Because of the steep reduction in federal funds for our national parks, the Smokies park has organized volunteer help for the purposes of monitoring the trails, correcting minor conditions such as briars and shrub growth, and reporting on washouts and blowdowns, which block trails on occasion. If you live near the park and are interested in this trail-maintenance effort, please phone park headquarters, (423) 436–1200, for information.

Fifth and also for the better, as are the previous two changes, is the Ridge-Runner project. Sixty-eight of the roughly 2,100 miles of the Appalachian Trail run through the Great Smoky Mountains National Park. With summer hikers and through-hikers (those attempting the full distance), the trail and shelters are heavily used. To assist hikers and to aid in keeping the trail and shelters clean, two ridge runners and several shelter caretakers are hired for the summer months. They have radios to call for assistance in emergencies. The ridge runners are hired by the Appalachian Trail Conference, the Smoky Mountains Hiking Club, and the Great Smoky Mountains Natural History Association to protect this segment of the Appalachian Trail and those who walk it.

You can contribute to the maintenance of the park by not interfering with nature. Instead of picking flowers or littering, interrupting or destroying the course of nature, learn to appreciate it. You should leave the park exactly as it was when you came. And do not feed any animals!

On Walking

We have written this book to share our experiences in the Great Smokies with other walkers who don't consider walking an athletic feat. It is intended for people who do not want to carry heavy backpacks or spend nights on the trail and those who have small children in tow or want a comfortable bed and good meal at night. It is also for those who seek the peace, quiet, and inspiration that come from a walk in the forest (which is what these Great Smokies offer).

Since almost all the trails head into the mountains, they go up. They do this with amazing ingenuity, usually at a reasonable rate of ascent and often following alongside streams. There are over 600 miles of streams, which drain mountain water down through coves. The trails following alongside provide natural paths through the woods.

The interlocking system of trails within the park seems to imply the need for rather long hikes—or a second car for hikes that start in one place and end in another. But we have not found this to be the case. We have been limited in time and endurance to relatively short walks, so we walk out on a trail and retrace our footsteps and find we enjoy doing this.

There is a technique to walking, and surprisingly few hikers have learned it. Many people pound their heels into the ground when walking. The human spinal column was never meant to be hammered by an endless succession of jolts transmitted by heels. Be conscious, when you are learning to walk properly, that the big muscles of your thighs should carry your body weight. Your knees should bend slightly, and your head and back should lean forward.

Roll onto the balls of your feet and push your weight forward with your toes. Develop an easy, slow, rhythmic pace. Allow your body to swing, not drag behind.

Wear comfortable clothes. Cotton, wool, and the new breathable outdoor fabrics are more comfortable than synthetics and not as sticky when climbing and expending a considerable amount of effort. Do not even contemplate walking in these hills in street shoes. Work or hiking boots are in order. Shoes should be well broken in and sturdy. Wear two pairs of socks. If you haven't discovered such things in the footcare department as innersoles and foam and moleskin padding plasters, check into them at once. Learn the art of soaking your feet, and pamper these vital appendages.

It rains frequently in the Smokies, so always carry some kind of rain gear. A lightweight poncho is easy to pack. Be certain that whatever rain gear you bring permits circulation of air but at the same time repels water.

Consider carrying a small pair of binoculars. A ten-power hand lens will also allow you to look more closely at flowers and other objects, revealing the details in a wonderful world of close-ups. We wear pedometers—they are not always precise, but are still helpful.

Carry drinking water from a safe source with you. Do not drink from any surface waters unless the water has been boiled at least one minute or has been given adequate chemical treatment.

TRAIL DESCRIPTIONS

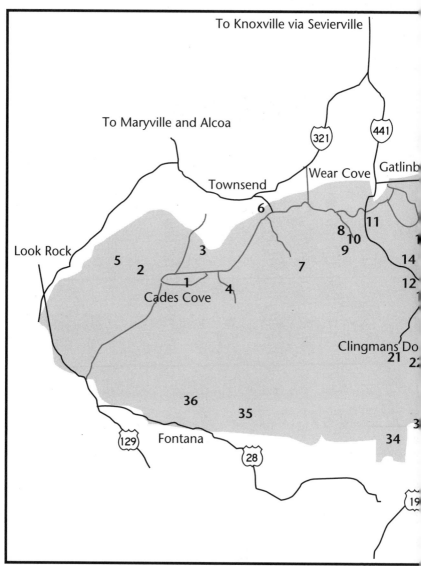

Location of Walks

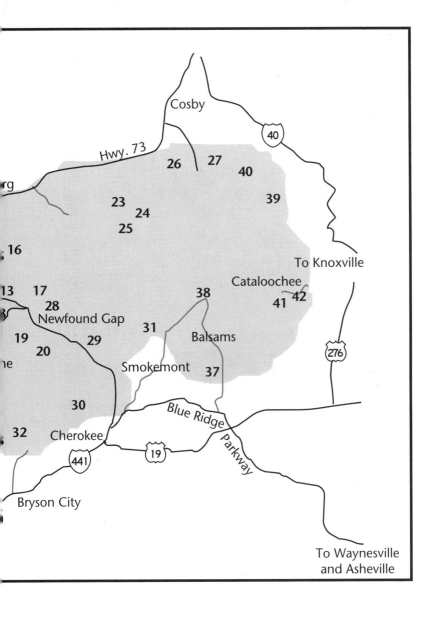

Deer Crossing in Cades Cove

Cades Cove Area

1. Cades Cove Loop
2. Abrams Falls
3. Rich Mountain Loop
4. Leadbetter Ridge–Russell Field Trail
5. Little Bottoms

Other Walks: Gregory Ridge Trail, Spence Field Trail, Gregory Bald Trail, Boundary Trail

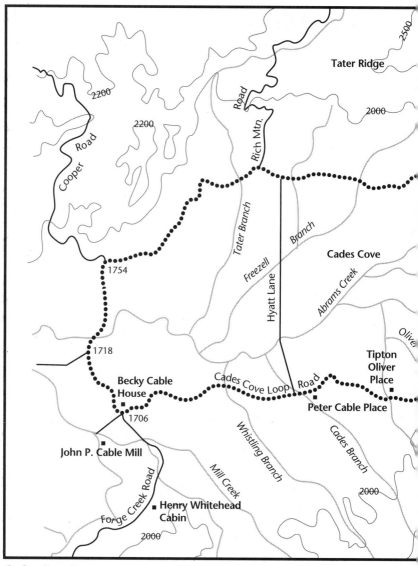

Cades Cove Loop

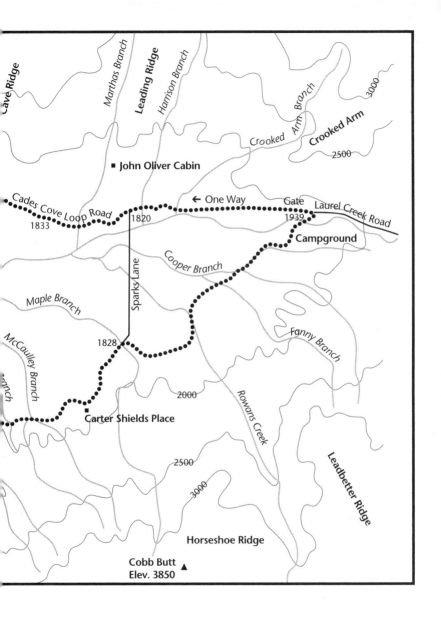

1. CADES COVE LOOP

Distance: 11-mile loop
Difficulty: Easy (bike ride)
Elevation: Road coasts 223 feet down to about the midpoint in the loop at the bridge crossing of Abrams Creek (1,939 feet to 1,716 feet). From here on, same elevation is regained as was lost; however, there are steep, but short, rises.
How to get there: Trail begins where the Cades Cove Loop Road starts, just beyond the campground turnoff.

The 11-mile Cades Cove Loop Road can be walked, but we especially recommend doing it by bicycle. The time you save can then be spent in leisurely exploration of the points of interest that you notice all along the way. Rental bikes are available for a modest fee at the Cades Cove Campground store. Remember to observe the rules of the road, and be extra cautious if you travel at peak traffic season. Wagon rides and traffic-free times are available; check with the Park Service for schedules.

The trip starts and finishes at Cades Cove Campground and goes through one of the stunning sights of the park—an upland valley with broad pastures and grazing cattle. The whole cove is encircled by tall wooded peaks that are enveloped in the blue mist that makes a perfect frame for such a pastoral setting.

The area has been developed by the National Park Service as a living museum in order to preserve some aspects of the mountain culture. And it does so with distinction. Only a half dozen mountain cabins, an old frame house, a few barns, a gristmill, and three churches are standing. They are all very discreetly underplayed, giving precedence to the natural wonder of the place. Almost one hundred families once lived in the cove without electricity. Several now live nearby and raise their cattle here. It is a showplace, with inspiring vistas. One may have the pleasure of imagining what satisfaction there must have been in discovering this wide and fertile valley.

In mid-May yellow poplar trees are in blossom. The roadsides are ablaze with golden ragwort, oxeye daisy, and yellow hop clover—all blooming with delightful casualness. We were pleased to be able to inspect the Mill Creek Dam, the floodgates, flume, and mechanism of the John P. Cable Mill. We came home with a small bag of stone-ground cornmeal purchased at the Cades Cove Visitor Center. By following the recipe on the bag, we had a delicious spoonbread at supper time.

We sat a spell on the lawn outside the Henry Whitehead place, secluded up a spur road a short distance from the mill. It was a very restful day. The only noise to disturb us came from the cicadas, which only lent the background music that recalls the agricultural heritage we all share.

Note: You might consider arranging for your bicycles the evening before you plan to make this circuit, for the rental office does not open until 9:00 A.M. An early morning start into the Cove might give you the special excitement of seeing the deer and wild turkey that often feed here at that time; it also reduces the hazards of heavy auto traffic later in the day.

2. ABRAMS FALLS

Distance: 5 miles (in and out)
Difficulty: Moderate
Elevation: Trail loses 310 feet as it follows Abrams Creek 2.5 miles downstream to the falls (1,710 feet to 1,400 feet). It is not downhill all the way, however, because it climbs over three descending ridges and slopes en route.
How to get there: Trail begins at the wooden bridge at the end of the parking area on the gravel side road at the west end of Cades Cove. (Take Cades Cove Loop Road.)

Get out on this trail early because then only a fisherman or two will be afoot, and you will have the path to yourself. The trail is popular and easy to reach, so it attracts numerous visitors.

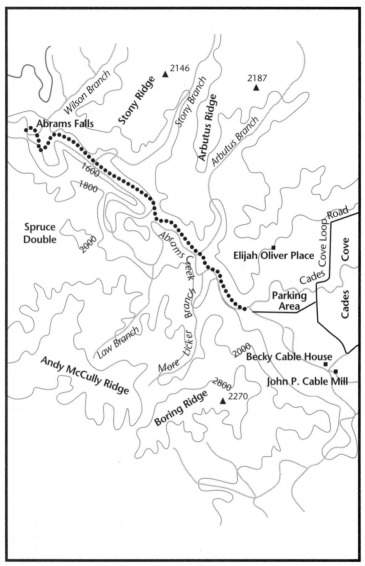

Abrams Falls

Abrams Creek is the sole drainage for the Cades Cove area and eventually empties into the Little Tennessee River. It moves rapidly along, dropping over a series of ledges, and looks like very pretty spillways. In early morning, the mist rises from the waters of the creek, and the tall dark hemlocks stand hushed in diffused light. Its water is crystal clear, but unlike many other streams in the park, its bottom is silt, giving an illusion of cloudiness that disappears when you look closer.

The pathway is broad and soft beneath your feet. It ascends and descends but is never precipitous. You cross over Abrams Creek on the bridge from the parking area and continue downstream through a tunnel of rhododendron. Here you can imagine you are walking in an arboretum, because the first quarter mile is so level. Expect to start an ascent right after the second log bridge—the first of three fairly easy slopes up which you must make your way.

The path of Abrams Creek veers sharply to the left and makes a big loop around the mass of Arbutus Ridge before continuing in its westerly direction. That is why you have to start climbing. Don't worry—the creek returns, and shortly you will be following along-side.

We walked here in May when the hemlocks were getting their spring growth and all their graceful branches were tipped with pale green. The huge, pale, pink clusters of mountain laurel dominated the scene. The foliage along the path makes it clear that at every season there are special attractions here. There is an abundance of trailing arbutus along the trail—hence the name of Arbutus Ridge. We were late to see its bloom. Galax and partridgeberry are here in quantity, as is wild bleeding heart, which covers a rocky projection. As we gained the top of the ridge to cross through the gap, we came upon a lovely view and found this a good place to stop and catch our breath.

You come across a fourth bridge over a Wilson Branch coming in from your right 2.5 miles up the trail. The water glides over a wide, dark rock and swirls out into Abrams Creek, creating still another perfect picture. It took us just an hour and a half to come this distance. And here, down a side trail and across another log bridge, is Abrams Falls, the destination of this walk.

The Abrams Creek water passes over an escarpment and plunges 20 feet into a large pool. Its sheer volume coming over the rock, with the rising mist, makes Abrams Falls impressive as you turn to look at it. Because of the slick rocks, it is very dangerous to go close to the top of the falls. People swim here in summer; if you choose to swim, be careful of currents and sharp rocks.

3. RICH MOUNTAIN LOOP
Distance: 7.5 miles (loop)
Difficulty: Strenuous
Elevation: Climb is 1,766 feet (1,920 feet to 3,686 feet), gains 1,500 feet within the first 2 miles, then gradually follows contours to the summit. Returning is similar, but by a different route.
How to get there: Trail begins just past the interpretive display building at the beginning of the Cades Cove Loop Road. Park before the one-way loop road starts and walk past the gate.

The days of the fire tower are over, since it is now easier and more efficient to spot fires and give instructions from the air. But the places where they stood, or in some instances still stand, are often sites of eminence in surroundings of wilderness. Rich Mountain Tower, now torn down, stood upon such a site. The mountain affords a commanding view of the cove and the mountains that surround it.

This circular walk is described here in a counterclockwise direction, beginning with the Crooked Arm Ridge Trail, which is 0.5 mile from the trailhead. A sign there points straight ahead for the loop trail; but to follow our path, take a right at Crooked Arm Branch. Either way, you return to this point and experience the same terrain and scenery.

The trail starts out through woods alongside one of the beautiful cove pastures, crosses the creek, and continues along it. It is an

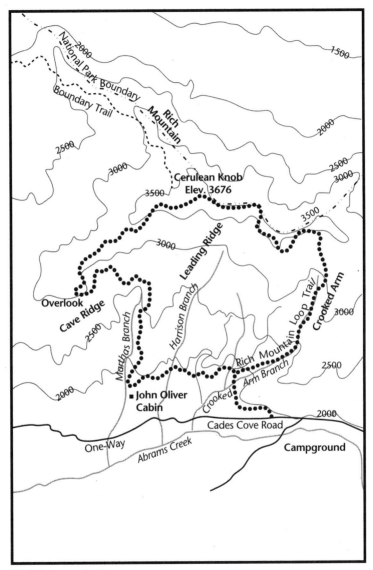

Rich Mountain Loop

unusual streambed with long reaches where it glides over solid rock. One more crossing of the creek and then the trail turns away to run in a series of switchbacks up the side of Rich Mountain, where it tops out near an open ledge for a rest stop. Considering the rise, this trail is really not difficult because of the way it is engineered. There are fine views into Cades Cove on the left and Tuckaleechee Cove on the right.

The trail, running slightly downhill, now follows a service road close to the northern border of the park. We had lunch in the tower clearing. As we rested there in the grass, we suddenly realized that the flitting motion in the oak tree above our heads was a hummingbird. Later, higher in the same tree, a crested flycatcher swooped in to rest for a moment.

The loop continues along a smooth road that feels like a boulevard. Two vistas afford spectacular views of Cades Cove and the mountains. In May and June this area has its share of flowering shrubs and wildflowers. In autumn the hardwoods are ablaze with color. And we are told that it is even handsome in winter, with the trees in hoarfrost. In late February you may find trailing arbutus in bloom.

After this, the downward trek becomes steep, rocky, and chopped up by horses in the seepage areas. It crosses three small streams and follows down the third, Martha's Branch. You ford it several times and come out behind the John Oliver place, 2.5 miles from the tower. Be sure to turn left here above the split-rail fence and climb away from the cabin. The trail will take you back to the starting point.

An alternate way to reach the tower site, only 5.4 miles and less of a climb, goes from the gap on the Rich Mountain gravel road off the Cades Cove Loop Road. This appeals to many walkers and is an in-and-out walk. The problem is that the road is one-way, and once on it, you must continue all the way to Townsend.

4. LEADBETTER RIDGE–RUSSELL FIELD TRAIL

Distance: 6 miles (up and back)

Difficulty: Moderate

Elevation: Climb is approximately 1,650 feet in 3 miles (1,965 feet to just over 3,600 feet). Over the first 2.5 miles trail gains 1,000 feet gradually. A final 650 feet in a half mile steepens the grade.

How to get there: Trail begins at the east end and at the top of the Cades Cove Picnic Area, behind a gated road. (The signs are for Spence and Russell fields.)

From the Cades Cove Campground the Leadbetter Ridge looms up behind, like a stage backdrop. It seems a natural to climb—as though there should be a spectacular view of Cades Cove from the top. If you climb it in this expectation, you will be disappointed, because there are no openings in the trees to allow you to look down. The best offered is an occasional glimpse of Thunderhead. But it is a popular walk anyway, one we found pleasant and comfortable and to be recommended.

It starts out as a wide and spacious, though rocky, service road that runs past a horse camp. For the first 1.5 miles it follows the course of Anthony Creek upstream through very dense woods where there were once farms. It is now all second growth. Evidences of this today are the lighter places in the woods and the exotic plants, like periwinkle myrtle. There are two substantial bridges, and after the second bridge at 1.5 miles, you turn with the Russell Field Trail, marked as it goes right.

Now you will penetrate deep into a cove of mature hardwoods, and as you go farther, larger trees appear. Fine specimens of eastern hemlock and yellow poplar mingle with maple, oak, magnolia, and holly of dimensions city dwellers would find hard to believe. This cove must receive a great deal of rainfall for the trees to reach these proportions. Not only are fallen trees covered deep in moss, but trunks of the live ones are as well. Stones and boulders in the brook are green with moss too. Lichen and leaf mold are redolent of the dampness of the ages. In April and May there are especially

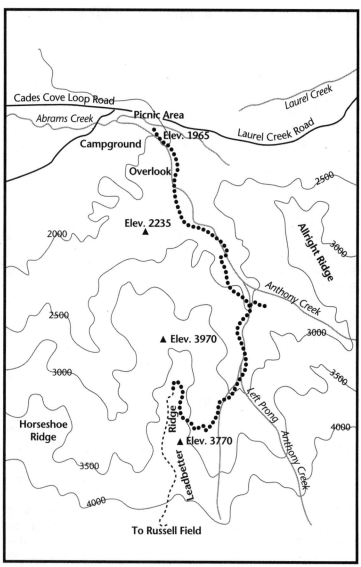

Leadbetter Ridge–Russell Field Trail

good stands of showy orchis and crested dwarf iris. The leaves of many other plants give evidence that flowers bloom here throughout the season.

If you could choose your weather for this trail, our advice would be to go after a big rain when the clouds are beginning to break up. When the rays of sunlight do appear, they seem literally to pierce the forest canopy and spotlight the glistening leaves in a most theatrical way. Indian pipes, ghostly, translucent flowers without chlorophyll, grow in colonies in summer. There are mushrooms, and toadstools so enormous they could shelter several small trolls.

At the far end of the cove the trail turns right, leaves the stream, and starts to climb up Leadbetter Ridge. This is what we did before turning around. Laurel and table mountain pine grow here, and there are occasional peek-through vistas southeastward to Thunderhead and the Smokies' main ridge. (Were you to continue to Russell Field, you could not expect a great view either as it is quite overgrown. That distance to Russell Field would be 10 miles round trip.)

5. LITTLE BOTTOMS

Distance: 5 miles (in and out)

Difficulty: Moderate. However, this is a narrow trail and should not be attempted by anyone who is not strong and sure of foot.

Elevation: Abrams Creek Campground is at an elevation of 1,120 feet; the back-country campsite is at 1,240 feet. The trail reaching it is 2 miles long, climbing up and over two hills about 1,400 feet high. From the campsite we climbed Hatcher Mountain Trail another half mile to an elevation of 1,750 feet.

How to get there: Trail begins at the far end of the Abrams Creek Campground, beyond a gated road. Hikers must park near the Abrams Creek Ranger Station 0.4 mile before the campground.

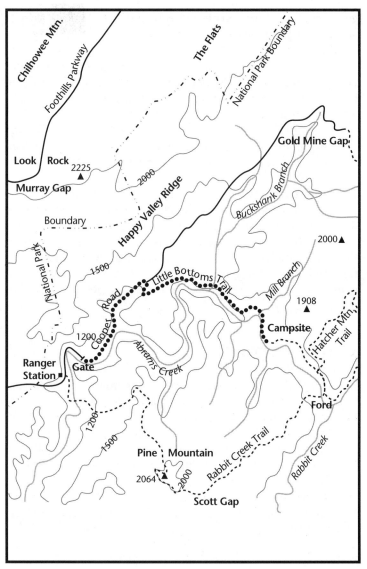

Little Bottoms

Here is a trail that encourages the sorting out of your thoughts, hopes, and aspirations. It is a quiet woodland walk from the Abrams Creek Campground. It runs along the lower section of Abrams Creek, the same stream along which you walk going to Abrams Falls from Cades Cove. The creek drains Cades Cove and winds its way westward through the northwest corner of the park. Here you will find the Abrams Creek Ranger Station.

Starting north out of the campground, follow Cooper Road for a mile on a service road through a dark grove of tall hemlocks, which scatter the sunlight into beautiful small patches of shimmering light. Abrams Creek on the right turns away after approximately a half mile. Don't worry, you will find it again. Ford two shallow streams and look for the National Park Service trail marker at one mile. Turn right as directed onto the Little Bottoms Trail.

You must pay attention to your footing. It is not strenuous, but occasionally there is a steep drop. The trail climbs for a quarter of a mile, and as you reach the top, you hear faithful Abrams Creek gurgling below on your right. You descend to stream level, go through dense woods, and, at a distance of 2.5 miles, come upon the back-country campsite at Little Bottoms—National Park Service No. 17.

From the campsite, after about 400 yards, you cross a brook. The trail then rises sharply onto a rocky ledge covered with laurel and pine, open in places to the sun. We sat here and ate our lunch, watching the lovely little parula warbler selecting bits of old man's beard lichen for a nesting material.

Although this is a good place to turn around, you can go ahead, as we did, to a junction about a mile farther, turn left, and walk along the side of Hatcher Mountain. This is a bit of a climb, but there are some modest views. If you continue right at the junction, the trail goes back down to the creek. It is possible (if the creek is low enough to ford safely) to go back to the ranger station via Scott Gap, following the Hannah Mountain Trail to the gap. The return would be 4 miles, making a total walk of 8 miles. You should check with the ranger before attempting this.

25

It was Memorial Day weekend when we walked this trail. The campground was full, but we saw practically no one all day on the sunny banks of the creek in this off-the-beaten-track corner of the park. Keeping your eyes down because of the narrowness of the trail is an asset, thus to focus on some of the handsome wildflowers that grow here. We saw the unusual colic root, a member of the lily family, the colorful, everlasting sweet pea, and the striking purple bull thistle.

The uphill and downhill portions of this walk make for equable walking. The return will take about the same time as coming in. It is particularly recommended to more adventurous walkers.

Other Walks

(Ask the Park Service for details.)

From 1,929 feet to 2,800 feet on the **Gregory Ridge Trail** (from a turnaround on Forge Creek Road, Cades Cove) is one of the more popular trails in the park—a round-trip distance of 3 miles in a mixed hardwood forest. It can be extended to climb along the Gregory Ridge to the Smokies crest—10 miles round-trip to Gregory Bald, 9 miles round-trip to Rich Gap.

Spence Field is a round trip of 11 miles (2,922-foot climb) and can be reached by continuing on the Anthony Creek Trail (Walk 5) and the Bote Mountain Trail.

Gregory Bald is a well-publicized grassy bald, with an outstanding display of flame azalea. The shortest trail is 7.8 miles (2,780 feet to 4,949 feet) round-trip from the one-way Parsons Branch Road (closed in winter).

Walks are possible on the **Boundary Trail**, off the one-way Rich Mountain Road (closed in winter) at Rich Gap; to the west, toward Ace Gap, and to the east, toward Rich Mountain. This trail is reached from the Rich Mountain Road turnoff from the north side of the Cades Cove loop along a delightfully twisting old mountain road, which long served as the main route to Cades Cove.

Townsend–Tremont Area

6. Chestnut Top Trail
7. Middle Prong–Greenbrier Ridge
Other Walks: Panther Creek Trail, Bote Mountain Trail, Lead Cove Trail, Lumber Ridge Trail, West Prong Trail

Mountain Laurel Blooms

6. CHESTNUT TOP TRAIL

Distance: 5 miles

Difficulty: Moderate

Elevation: Vertical rise is 1,200 feet in 2.5 miles (1,160 feet to 2,360 feet). Trail climbs rather sharply through a spring flower garden, almost 500 feet in a half mile, then gradually achieves the top.

How to get there: Trail begins off the Townsend Road, near the wye, just where the highway divides. The Townsend Road is TN Route 73, and the entry is about 100 yards north of its junction with the Little River Road, on the western side of the Townsend Road at a gap in a rail fence.

This is a walk along a portion of the northern boundary of the park, easily accessible from the road entering the park. It follows a popular trail ending in 4.5 miles at Schoolhouse Gap.

Examine a map of the perimeter of the park and you will see that there are few opportunities to patrol its borders. Parts of the perimeter are covered by old dirt roads, and where there are trails, they have often fallen into chaotic condition through low maintenance. But this stretch westward from the Townsend Road is in good shape. It is a narrow footpath. It ascends slowly, switching back after gaining a height that affords a good view down onto Townsend. It then follows along Chestnut Top "Lead" (as it is called locally), a ridge from which you are able to get occasional glimpses of Tuckaleechee Cove to the north and of the main ridge of the Appalachians to the south. Because it is a high ridge trail, you do not walk alongside streams noisily dashing against rocks. It is narrow and quiet—a pathway along the ridge through sandy, pine-covered territory. It is good walking and known for wildflowers in the spring, when we took this trail.

We walked single file because the trail goes up through dense woods along a steep slope. It climbs gradually up over the rocky ledges seen from the highway. Mosses, lichens, and ferns as well as numbers of wildflowers grow on the steep slope. At the time we traveled, beds of partridgeberry were in flower. Galax was at its

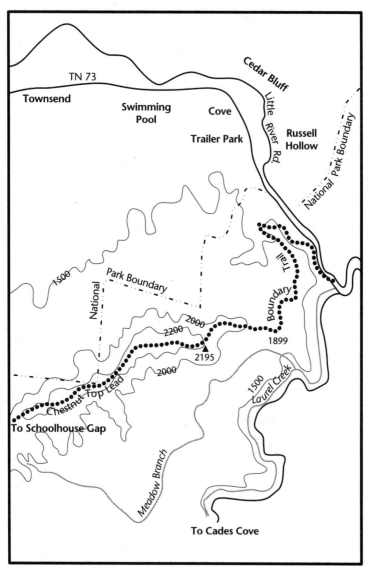

Chestnut Top Trail

height. Farther up we saw Bowman's root and pink lady's slipper. There is also considerable poison ivy along the beginnings of the trail, so take care. Many flowers, such as hepatica, trillium, jack-in-the-pulpit, and bloodroot, bloom earlier here than on nearby trails because of the exposed slope.

We located a small warbler identified by the bold head striping—one stripe right through the eye—and its repeated trilling song. The bird book helped us identify it as the worm-eating warbler. Although we cannot promise you will see one just here, you will surely be rewarded if you keep looking, because birds are creatures of habit and are territorial. A second growth of deciduous woodlands on a hillside, such as this, is the worm-eating warbler's most commonly preferred habitat. He is not terribly active, and you are most likely to see him low in the branches when you hear his trill and twittery song.

At just about a half mile the trail turns abruptly to the left, around a rock outcrop. As it does you get the good view into Townsend. It then levels out and winds around behind the hills for another half mile before starting to climb up to the ridge. The distance we covered in two hours was just about 3 miles on our pedometers, and we had topped the crest and walked a bit beyond before turning back.

7. MIDDLE PRONG–GREENBRIER RIDGE

Distance: 10 miles (up and back)
Difficulty: Moderate to strenuous
Elevation: This well-graded old road gains 2,074 feet in 5 miles (1,926 feet to 4,000 feet). (You need walk only as far as you choose for a turnaround.) Even the shortest walk is pleasant, because you start out in one of the more remote areas of the park. Here are alternate objectives along this trail:

2.3 miles (one-way) to the trail marker of the Panther Creek Trail—the trail to Jakes Gap, starting on the opposite side of the creek (2,600 feet).

31

1.8 miles (one-way) to the next trail marker—at the junction of Lynn Camp Prong Trail to Miry Ridge and Greenbrier Ridge Trail to Sams Gap and Derrick Knob.

5 miles (one-way) to the 3,700-foot elevation on the Greenbrier Ridge.

8.3 miles (one-way) to Sams Gap (4,780 feet) and the Appalachian Trail.

How to get there: Trail begins at the end of the Tremont Road. From Townsend turn onto Laurel Creek Road (toward Cades Cove) after entering the park. Less than a quarter mile from this junction, Tremont Road leads south, coming to the Great Smoky Mountains Institute at Tremont (GSMIT) in 2 miles (gate here is closed in winter); in 5.5 miles of gravel road to a second gate and turnaround.

Just beyond the footbridge is a trail marker reading: APPALACHIAN TRAIL, 8.1, JAKES GAP 5. It is intended for backpackers and might confuse a walker. In Marks Cove is a back-country campsite, one of nearly a hundred scattered along the trails within the park. A permit must be obtained to use one. (Most likely the backpacker will continue on to another campsite and Miry Ridge is a route to others.) All trail junctions are well marked. As the trail along Greenbrier Ridge ends at Sams Gap on the Appalachian Trail, it is so marked at junctions ahead.

The drive into the Tremont area, alongside the Middle Prong, an enchanting stream away from crowds, is one of the attractive features of this trip. The area was cut over by the Little River Lumber Company starting in the 1920s. They were still at it until the late 1930s, so very few trees were standing here when the park was formed. Now, under park management, it is recovering and returning to wilderness. The trail starts on an iron bridge and follows an old railroad bed, keeping to the west of Lynn Camp Prong for the first 3 miles. Then the Indian Flats Prong, coming down off the slopes, joins the river.

At this junction the trail turns south and continues alongside the Indian Flats Prong. Here it follows an old railroad logging bed,

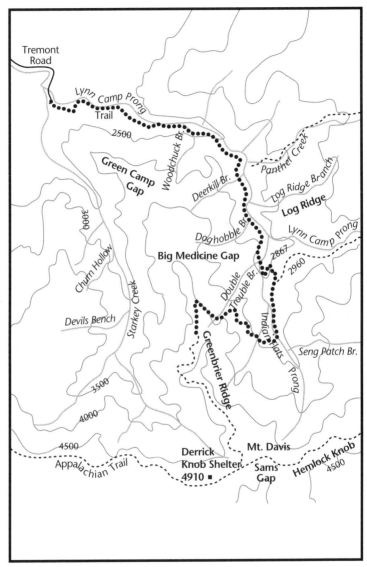

Middle Prong–Greenbrier Ridge

and the grade is not as steep. As you proceed, you see where they blasted rock to put that railroad through. The trail simply winds around the side of the mountain until it reaches the ridge. The footing is particularly good. There are several small streams to ford and one to cross on a log. Nearing the top of the ridge, views expand to the north. Rhododendron, laurel, leucothoe (doghobble), and the velvety Vasey's trillium grow along the path.

Other Walks

(Ask the Park Service for details.)

Panther Creek Trail to Jakes Gap and Miry Ridge Trail. (See Walks 7 and 9.) The trail starts 2.3 miles along Middle Prong Trail after fording Panther Creek. At high water this can be dangerous. Ask a ranger for advice. The round-trip to Jakes Gap from that point is 4.4 miles, climbing 1,500 feet. (Road closed off-season at GSMIT, which adds 7 miles to walk.)

Bote Mountain Trail. There are two ways to get to this dry ridge from Laurel Creek Road. The one closest to the Townsend wye is an old boulder-blocked service road known as the Bote Mountain Trail, but the second is a more secluded and picturesque path. It is the **Lead Cove Trail** and starts about 2 miles east of Cades Cove, a 1.7-mile walk to the ridge. (It is possible to climb and return via the Anthony Creek Trail.)

Lumber Ridge Trail out of the GSMIT along Lumber Ridge reaches Little Buckhorn Gap in 4.1 miles after climbing 1,150 feet.

West Prong Trail. There is a trail that climbs the side of Fodderstack Mountain from the GSMIT, then down to cross the West Prong. At 2.5 miles, you reach the Bote Mountain Road.

Elkmont Area

8. Meigs Mountain Trail
9. Jakes Creek Trail to Miry Ridge Overlook
10. Cucumber Gap
11. Huskey Gap
Other Walks: Sugarland Mountain Trail, Laurel Falls Trail, Curry Mountain Trail, Meigs Creek Trail

Walks 8, 9, and 10 all begin at the same place—the gate on the Jakes Creek Road, at the end of a row of summer cottages. (These cottages, formerly under the auspices of the Appalachian Club, have reverted to park ownership; some will be removed and others may be remodeled for park use.) There is parking along the road outside the gate. To reach this gate in your car, you must turn toward the Elkmont Campground, south from the Little River Road. Just at the campground entrance, the road forks. Continue ahead on the left fork, making a slight climb. There is a sign showing JAKES CREEK TRAIL 1 MILE. Follow this road until it splits, and then take the right fork 0.5 mile to the trailhead.

Grotto Falls

8. MEIGS MOUNTAIN TRAIL

Distance: 5 miles (in and out)

Difficulty: Easy

Elevation: Trail is fairly level, following the contour of the hillsides, after an initial climb of 300 feet from the parking lot (2,350 feet to 2,650 feet).

How to get there: Trail begins approximately 1.5 miles south of the Elkmont Campground entrance. (See page 35 for directions to trailhead.) There is a gate at the end of this road (Jakes Creek Road). From here the Jakes Creek and Cucumber Gap Trails also start. The parking area allows for a dozen or more cars.

This is an easy trail within anyone's capabilities. It is a nice walk to linger along. Pleasant and quiet, it meanders as though headed nowhere, whereas it actually follows an old roadbed lying about 2 miles from, and roughly parallel to, the Little River. In 1926 when people were scratching a living in these parts, it was the road to their homesteads. You will begin seeing evidence of this right away, because there were probably twenty families living here.

We walked about two and a half hours with no particular goal in mind and had come 2.5 miles. The return trip took us just over an hour. It is possible to set about any pace you want. The trail eventually joins the Meigs Creek Trail, which turns north and leads after 8.5 miles to a deep pool along the Little River, which is known as "the Sinks." You need not be concerned about the distance. Look at your watch and turn around whenever you wish.

In the first mile the trail passes through deep hollows. More than a dozen descending rivulets from springs higher up cross the trail. But you can hop over them effortlessly. Starting at the gate there is a climb of less than a half mile. Then, just beyond the trail marker indicating the Cucumber Gap Trail on the left, the trail reaches a fork. Take the Meigs Mountain Trail to the right. After another .25 mile, it crosses the creek on a log bridge and continues along lower slopes of the mountainside.

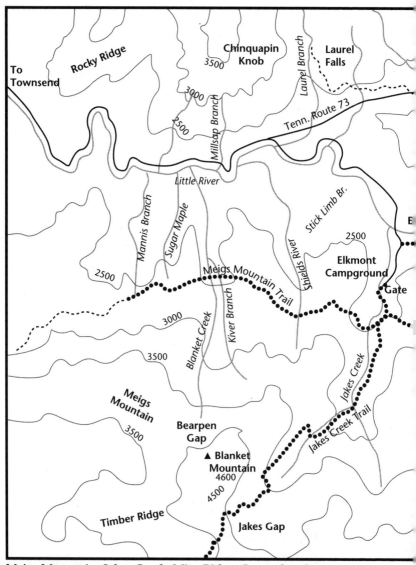

Meigs Mountain, Jakes Creek, Miry Ridge, Cucumber Gap,
and Huskey Gap

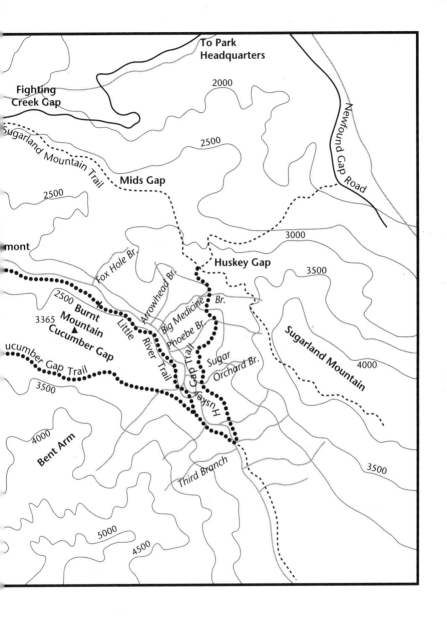

The disintegrated foundations of several dwellings appear here amidst stands of daffodils, rusty iron castings, and carpets of periwinkle myrtle. In this stillness you may wonder if the tranquility of these surroundings made the drudgery and endless chores that faced the settlers more bearable. We came to a place where a stream had been dammed, probably for a cool place to keep butter and milk. This was our turnaround.

We decided almost anything can be concealed within these woods. Hoofprints told us from their depth and spacing that a deer had bounded off not long before we came, and we imagined that it stood watching us. The insistent ovenbirds with their crescendo calls seemed to be stationed all along the way. Thrushes were easily heard, though we did not see them. Two little creatures caught our eye just by chance: A small brown snake stretched out like a fallen twig remained motionless as we examined it while a salamander poised suspended on a boulder for an instant and then escaped.

On the way back, as the path crossed between two larger hills and through a gap, we heard a pileated woodpecker stuttering. Its call was anguished and it seemed insulted when we came near its haunts (though it may well be a great pretense).

Some trails in the Smokies do not come to a spectacular overlook, but they are most enjoyable because they do not attract the crowds. Meigs Mountain is such a trail.

9. Jakes Creek Trail to Miry Ridge Overlook

Distance: 8 miles (up and back)
Difficulty: Strenuous
Elevation: Trail presents a 4-mile vertical rise of 2,350 feet (2,259 feet to 4,609 feet). It is well graded.
How to get there: Trail begins at gate on Jakes Creek Road, same as Walks 8 and 10. (For directions to trailhead, see page 35.)

When you consider this hike as a 4-mile climb up combined with a 4-mile coast down, then the total 8 miles seems an acceptable distance if spread over a full day's walk. It is, in a way, a challenging one because the rise is 2,350 feet. The rewards are in the view from the ridgetop and the sense of accomplishment on reaching it. If you take care to pace yourself properly and make frequent rest stops, this walk will leave you feeling like a champ. Of course, you do not have to go all the way unless you want to.

Starting off as Walks 8 and 10 do, Jakes Creek Trail continues on the old road after the other trails have veered off. This road has been cut into the steep mountainside that forms the ravine drained by Jakes Creek. It is broad, but inexorably uphill, and is an excellent roadway to the point where it fords Newt Prong, a good-sized creek. No problem—there are plenty of stepping stones. Lean against a tree and take a few breaths here. You have come about a mile and a half.

Now the road narrows, and grass grows in its center. The footing is softer and the ascent gentler. As it travels and hugs the mountainside, there are ravishing views of the plummeting, cascading torrent on the right. In some places dark rhododendrons bend over deep pools. In other places the water rushes between great gray boulders.

At just over halfway up, there is another crossing by hop, skip, and jump over water. This is a good place for another breather because after this the path gets steeper and the forest becomes thinner. There is one switchback, a number of small waterways to cross, and a back-country campsite, Lower Jakes Gap, before you reach the gap.

Miry Ridge Trail goes left from the trail junction at Jakes Gap. This is a very nice part of the journey—first through open forest carpeted with wildflowers, then through shady hemlock. The final section of the trip leads through a rhododendron tunnel and up to an open ridgetop with excellent views of Lynn Camp Prong Valley and Mellinger Death Ridge. The ridges on the horizon form the crest of the Smokies with the Appalachian Trail running along them. Rocks to the left provide a beautiful lunch spot surrounded by Catawba rhododendron and mountain laurel. These evergreen shrubs bloom in May or early June.

Except for the knees, which take the jolts as you go downhill, the return is a breeze. As you leave these higher elevations, look for the Canada warbler. In spring the Fraser magnolia fills the air with its heavy scent. The little streams that cross the path provide a blessed coolness all along the way.

10. CUCUMBER GAP

Distance: 5 miles (out and back)
Difficulty: Easy
Elevation: About 2,550 feet at both ends of trail. In the middle, at Cucumber Gap—3,000 feet.
How to get there: Trail begins at gate on Jakes Creek Road, same as Walks 8 and 9. (See page 35 for directions.)

Cucumber Gap is the saddle between Burnt Mountain, just south of Elkmont Campground, and the Bent Arm of the Miry Ridge. The trail through the gap climbs so very gradually that you are scarcely aware of having gained 450 feet as it begins to descend to the Little River Trail. We suggest you follow the trail eastward as it comes up the old road from the gate at the end of Jakes Creek Road. At 0.3 mile the trail turns abruptly left and crosses a little creek known as Tulip Branch. It travels through a forest of evergreens and deciduous trees, most of which have grown up since logging operations finally ceased here.

Lumbering in this area extended from the 1800s up until 1938, when all operations finally ceased. At first big logs were pulled out by an ox team and then floated down the river. Word eventually spread about the tremendous size of the trees here, and big-time operators moved in. At the beginning of the twentieth century the section of land from Clingmans Dome down to Tuckaleechee Cove in Townsend, Tennessee, was worked by the Little River Lumber Company. In its logging operations here it processed more than a half-billion board feet of lumber. From a single yellow poplar tree, over 100 feet high, the lumber company could have extracted as much as 18,000 board feet of timber.

The Little River Company was only one of the huge lumbering operations with settlements around the perimeter of what is now the national park. They worked at a fast pace. Rail lines were constructed, and the steep slopes were denuded. At the time there was little concern about the resultant erosion, the loss of humus, and the destruction of the magnificent forest. But for the establishment of the park, the forest would no longer have been able to reproduce itself. Those of us who use the forests now must realize the trust and observe the custodial responsibilities we have inherited.

On this trail you should surely hear the ovenbird, whose call is loud, clear, and repetitious. It is very easy to identify—only two notes repeated as many as ten times and usually described as saying "tea-cher, tea-cher, tea-cher." It is a heavy-bodied warbler that prefers dry deciduous woods like this. The ovenbird habitually stays very low in the understory or may be seen on the ground among leaves like a wood thrush. It has a streaked breast like a wood thrush, but its upper parts are olive, and it has an orange-brown patch on its head. Look carefully, because it often sings on an exposed branch in areas that are not too thick.

Cucumber Gap supports a wide variety of flowers in April, including bloodroot, spring beauty, trout lily, painted trillium Fraser's sedge, and dwarf ginseng. Wild turkey and deer roam through this area.

The trail comes out on the Little River Trail. You could walk north on it and make a one-way walk if you can work out the logistics of getting back to your car.

11. HUSKEY GAP

Distance: 9 miles (up and back)
Difficulty: Easy to moderate
Elevation: At the gate—2,120 feet. Following the trail for 4.5 miles along the Little River Valley and up the gradual slope of Sugarland Mountain leads to Huskey Gap—3,180 feet (1,060-foot rise).

How to get there: Trail begins at the gate at the beginning of the road up the Little River Valley. This road starts at the left fork by the Elkmont Campground and continues past several unoccupied summer cabins. The campground lies to the right of the road.

Huskey Gap, at 3,180 feet elevation, affords an east-west pass over the Sugarland Mountain Ridge 2.5 miles due south of the Park Headquarters. This walk to Huskey Gap follows an old road along the upper Little River Valley above Elkmont to connect with that east-west pass. The distance from the gate to the Huskey Gap Trail is 2.5 miles, and it is 2 miles more to the gap. It returns via the same route.

On that first stretch of the road along the turbulent river you have a good view of the hulk of Sugarland Mountain on the other side and its peak, which rises up to 4,833 feet. You will find several benches along the way. After 2 miles you will see the Cucumber Gap Trail coming down at an angle from the right. Then, about half a mile along, you cross to the other side of the river on a bridge. And after the bridge, in about 100 yards, the trail to Huskey Gap cuts off to the left. It starts off on the level from the road but rises quickly over a small hump of land and soon leads into a lovely, open, second-growth forest, with an understory of fledgling hemlock and a carpet of fern.

We saw these slopes after a rain. The forest was glistening. Each branch of hemlock, each frond of fern had its own gleaming droplets dangling and sparkling. The slanting early morning rays of sunlight caught every tiny branch. It was early May and there was a whole hillside of red wake-robin trilliums punctuated with yellow trillium or toadshade—dreary names for fabulous blooms. We also watched a pair of black-throated blue warblers building a nest, a tiny suspended cup that looked as though it were bound together with cobwebs. We looked closer at this tidy miracle of roots and hair so neatly wrought.

The trail is comfortable, for the footing is spongy leaf mold or pine needles. It climbs ever so gradually and is 2 miles to Huskey

Gap, a junction of the Sugarland Mountain and Huskey Gap trails. To the right Sugarland Mountain Trail leads 9 miles to the Appalachian Trail. Getting there is the attraction—walk along slowly. (It would be possible to continue on from the gap 2 miles and come out on the Newfound Gap Road at 1,800 feet, or turn west at the gap intersection on the Sugarland Mountain Trail, which leads 3 miles to Fighting Creek Gap, on the Little River Road, at 2,300 feet elevation. At 2.5 miles you reach an open area with a fine view of Sugarland Valley.)

Other Walks

(Ask the Park Service for details.)

Sugarland Mountain Trail begins on the Little River Road at Fighting Creek Gap about 4 miles west of the visitor center. It climbs 800 feet in 3 miles to Huskey Gap. (It continues from here along the mountain ridge another 9 miles to the Appalachian Trail near Mount Collins.)

Laurel Falls Trail begins on the Little River Road at Fighting Creek Gap (the same parking area as the Sugarland Mountain Trail). It runs 4 miles up to Cove Mountain fire tower, a climb of 1,780 feet. The trail marker points to Laurel Falls. That portion that leads you in 1.3 miles to Laurel Falls has been so heavily traveled that the National Park Service has put down an asphalt walkway.

Curry Mountain Trail leads south, opposite the Metcalf Bottoms picnic area on the Little River Road, to the Meigs Mountain Trail in 3.3 miles. The climb is through a hardwood forest and at 2 miles reaches Curry Gap between Curry He and Curry She, but there is no view, and it is another mile to the junction with the Meigs Mountain Trail.

Meigs Creek Trail leads south from "the Sinks" on the Little River Road, climbing more than 800 feet in 3.5 miles to connect with the Meigs Mountain Trail. Meigs Creek Trail has 18 creek crossings; bring water shoes, but don't try this trail in wet weather.

Chimney Tops

Gatlinburg–Mount Le Conte Area

12. Chimney Tops
13. Alum Cave Bluffs
14. Bull Head
15. Rainbow Falls
16. Grotto Falls
Other Walks: Appalachian–Boulevard Trail, Huskey Gap Trail, Boundary Trail, Baskins Creek Trail

12. CHIMNEY TOPS

Distance: 4 miles (up and back)

Difficulty: Moderate to strenuous

Elevation: Vertical rise is 1,350 feet in 2 miles (3,400 feet to 4,750 feet). Though short, this trail presents a challenge. The first mile up is fairly easy, but pace yourself for the rest of the trip.

How to get there: Trail begins at a designated parking area on the Newfound Gap Road. This is south of the Sugarland Park Headquarters about 7 miles and is on the west side of the road.

You will not be alone here, because a walk like Chimney Tops, which has a goal, is popular. In addition, the parking area for the walk is on the main road. People see the sign and other cars parked there. They may even notice the chimneys themselves as they drive along. Prepare to pant a little, to stop often, and to let others pass you by. The woods are beautiful the entire way. The reward is a fine view and a close look at these odd rock formations.

The trail starts out crossing two substantial creeks four times on bridges. Each crossing provides a different ambience. When you come upon the third bridge, it looks as though a Japanese water garden had been lifted and dropped into the Smokies, so artfully does the water fall between and over the ledges on the side. On the other side the boulders are immense and gray-green.

After the fourth bridge the trail splits, and the Chimney Tops Trail goes to the right. Just as we turned there, a bird flew across our path, flying low to the ground. An investigation of the bank it had flown from revealed the neat, comfortable nest of the junco, exquisitely woven from grasses and feathers and containing four tiny pale-green speckled eggs.

The way becomes steeper after this turn and gives you the excuse to slow down. We became particularly diligent in our search for birds. We heard the complicated trilling and many-noted song of the winter wren. Tiny and dun-colored as he is, he makes the finest music in these Tennessee–North Carolina woods. Until the naturalist at Sugarlands instructed us to look low or on the ground, we had not spotted one. This time we found him in the leaves near an old rotting log.

The path is wide and well traveled and switches back several times to bring you to the top. The ledge gets quite narrow with spectacular views across to Mount Le Conte and Balsam Point. The rock formation looks like highly polished slate. The National Park Service advises that to go beyond the view is dangerous. Further exploration is discouraged.

Mount Le Conte

Mount Le Conte, 6,593 feet, is the third highest peak within the park. It stands apart from the main ridge of the Appalachians and was named after Joseph Le Conte (1823–1901), a chemistry professor at the University of South Carolina who had spent some of his early years in the Appalachians and later was an early, enthusiastic member of the Sierra Club. (The mountain was named by Samuel Buckley, a natural scientist, on a trip of exploration in 1856, as were many of the peaks, including Clingmans Dome and Mount Guyot.)

Climbing Mount Le Conte is the traditional trip for mountain-climbing enthusiasts and many less athletic tourists. To make it up and back in a day is very strenuous for those unaccustomed to hiking. Those who plan ahead can spend the night at the lodge maintained at the top and return the next day. Meals and bedding are supplied, so all you need carry is a drink, snacks, warm clothes, and your raincoat. Be sure to make reservations at the lodge well in advance, as there are no casual services here. It is a popular spot in the vacation season and is booked up for months in advance.

We stayed at Le Conte Lodge and thought it rather primitive and with no feeling of the camaraderie usually associated with such hostelries. But these things change, we are told, and conditions do vary. You can make reservations at Le Conte Lodge by calling (423) 429–5704. It is a beautiful place on a clear night. If you walk out a quarter-mile to Cliff Top, you can see the lights of Knoxville twinkling off in the distance.

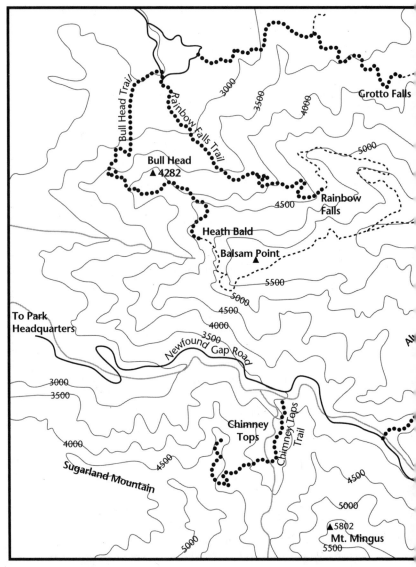

Le Conte Area Trails

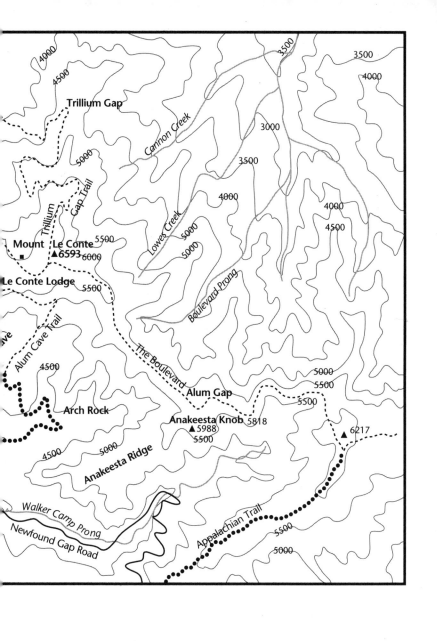

There are five different trails leading to Mount Le Conte. Walks 13, 14, 15, 16, and 17 (in the Newfound Gap–Clingmans Dome Area) describe the early portions of each one. We made the trip in on the Boulevard Trail, a continuation of Walk 17, which is the longest but least strenuous (8 miles). We came back on the Bull Head, Walk 14 (7.1 miles), with good views and massive rock formations.

13. ALUM CAVE BLUFFS

Distance: 5.1 miles (up and back)
Difficulty: Moderate
Elevation: Vertical rise is 1,400 feet in 2.25 miles (3,840 feet to 5,200 feet). Though short, trail presents a steady, gradual climb and an easy return.
How to get there: Alum Cave Trail begins on the Newfound Gap Road. It leaves from the parking place so marked and is just over 8.4 miles south of Sugarlands Visitor Center.

When we finally tackled this trail, we found it so engrossing that we took no notice of whether it was strenuous or not. We had been told not to miss Alum Cave Bluffs but were given the impression that it might be rather strenuous for us. It is certainly a march upward, but it is well engineered, quite safe, and just over 2 miles to the bluffs. We took four hours to go up and back, but allow more if you can. The trail includes points of geological interest, splendid views, worlds of rhododendron and laurel, and, in early spring, a wealth of warblers. We also identified the black-throated blue, the blackburnian, and the chestnut-sided, as well as the solitary vireo and veery.

You will notice immediately the devastation caused by the great precipitation of Labor Day 1951. In a matter of one hour the summit of Mount Le Conte was doused with four inches of rain. This turned Alum Cave Creek into a sluiceway. Great trees were wrenched up by their roots and tossed around like matchsticks.

Rocks and debris joined the tumbling torrent and forever changed the contours of the land. As a result, the path was completely rebuilt and is excellent. However, there are a great many spreading roots and rocks that you should watch for so that you don't trip over them.

In June 1993, a smaller cloudburst gouged a 35-foot trench out of the forest near Arch Rock. The devastation wrought will be marveled at for years to come.

The first half mile or so along the creek, the trail goes through tunnels of rhododendron and laurel. It crosses and recrosses Alum Cave Creek and two of its tributaries. At 1.3 miles it takes a right-hand turn across the creek once more into a large hole. This hole is the Arch Rock, an Anakeesta formation consisting of sandstone, slate, and phyllite. It is really a tunnel, and the grade of the path going through is very steep. A cable and steps help, but hiking traffic is one-way; wait for others to complete the tunnel before entering.

From this point the trail rises sharply and comes out on a table of rock covered with sand myrtle. It is a good place for a break—to have sandwiches and look out at the rippling ridges of Sugarland Mountain and Chimney Tops. To the west and higher up is a sharp ridge with a small window carved by erosion. Four peregrine falcon chicks fledged on this ridge in 1997, the first peregrines hatched in the park since 1942. Peregrines from other areas were reintroduced in the park during the 1980s. In 1998, three more chicks fledged.

After this breather it seems but a trifling matter to reach the Alum Cave, which is neither alum nor a cave. Rather, it is a tremendous bluff, so eroded by wind and weather as to have produced a cavelike overhang. If you touch a finger to the rock, the flake will taste salty and bitter. It is worthwhile to continue beyond these overhangs another 0.2 mile. Here is another and different view—this time toward the massive south face of Le Conte, scored by landslides of the past.

14. BULL HEAD

Distance: 6 miles (up and back)

Difficulty: Moderate

Elevation: Vertical rise is 2,020 feet in 3 miles (2,580 feet to 4,600 feet). Although the western flank, which the trail ascends, is quite steep (between 3,000 and 4,000 feet), the climb is gradual due to switchbacks.

How to get there: Trail begins from the parking lot on the loop of the Cherokee Orchard Road. To reach this, turn south onto Airport Road (at traffic light #8) from Main Street in Gatlinburg, then continue 3 miles past the Municipal Auditorium and by the Noah Ogle Place. It is here that the loop road begins. Take the right road 0.4 mile farther to the parking lot. The Bull Head Trail starts off as a gated service road on the right from here.

Bull Head is the first prominent peak southeast from the park headquarters at Sugarlands. You see it clearly on the model at the Sugarlands Visitor Center, which shows the topography of the surrounding area. Its steep slopes are those on your left about 2 miles after you leave these attractive buildings and drive south toward Newfound Gap. The Bull Head Trail to Mount Le Conte does not lead to Bull Head's peak. It climbs up and around it onto a ridge near the top that leads to Balsam Point and on dramatically to still higher elevations. The distance to Mount Le Conte is 7.1 miles. It is one of the most popular hiking routes because of the sweeping views to the west available from this high ridge.

If you are not easily discouraged by steep slopes, climbing these for about 2.5 miles can be rewarding. After leaving the parking area in Cherokee Orchard and the service road that leads the first half mile, the trail cuts off to the left. It soon gives one a sense of remoteness, of leaving civilization behind. The grade is gradual, and you gain your elevation by a series of switchbacks.

During wildflower season, the woods are particularly alive. Wildlife is plentiful, and the surroundings are verily mountainous with gray rock outcroppings, surfaced by mosses and lichens.

When you reach the treeless area near the ridge, you come to a heath and some large rocks. From here is a fine view down into Cherokee Orchard and beyond. There are also views west, and you can see the whole stretch of Sugarland Mountain as well as Blanket Mountain beyond. (You must continue on another half mile for the opening that allows this.)

15. RAINBOW FALLS

Distance: 5.4 miles (up and back)

Difficulty: Moderate

Elevation: Vertical rise is 1,750 feet in 2.5 miles (2,576 feet to 4,326 feet). Trail presents a steady, gradual climb and an easy return.

How to get there: Trail begins off the Cherokee Orchard Road, a one-way loop road just south of Gatlinburg, which you reach from the center of town (traffic light #8). There is ample parking. (See Walk 14.)

The name of this trail originates in the rainbow effect often achieved in afternoon sunlight as it strikes through the mist associated with the falls on Le Conte Creek here. Waters spill and drop free for about 80 feet over the lip of a wide rocky bastion at the end of the cove. This rock wall has a breadth probably double its height, whereas the stream of water as it tumbles from the top is narrow—less than 10 feet. The sight is a dramatic one.

The walk to the falls is very popular but is not easy. If you allow the time, the overall trip is not as bad as you are led to expect. The distance from the parking lot at Cherokee Orchard up to the falls is 2.7 miles. The return trip is all downhill. Despite a struggle to get up, it is definitely worth it.

After leaving the parking lot, the trail goes along the east side of Le Conte Creek. It is a well-graded trail, probably 4 feet wide, but starts climbing at once to reach the falls. Tree roots are exposed in many places, making the path generally rough because of

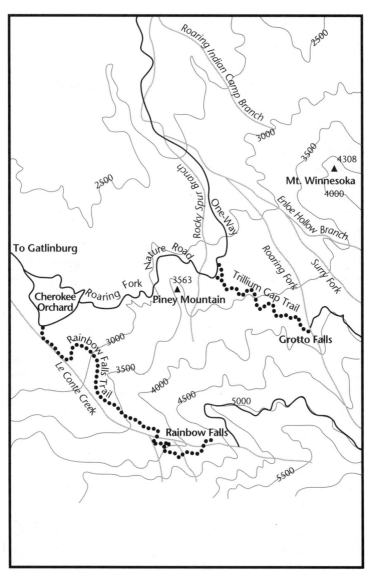

Rainbow Falls and Grotto Falls

the heavy use. It is high above the creek and well to the east and therefore goes through woods rather than alongside the streambed. This fine forest is full of noble trees making up one of the Smokies' big tree groves. It is easily reached and should make a lasting impression on you. There is a complement of wildflowers and a background of lilting music from the bosky stream.

The trail continues along the contour of the mountain. At 2 miles the trail proceeds at a more gradual slope up to the falls. These middle elevations from 2,500 feet to 4,500 feet can be delightful for bird-watching if you take it easy and walk slowly. The maple, oak, birch, and beech trees—common throughout the East and often seen as specimens—will surprise you. The trunks are larger, and the trees reach tremendous heights, standing close together as they do. One very common tree here is the mountain silverbell. You would do well to look up leaf and bark patterns before you take this walk.

Two log footbridges are at the falls. From the first one you can hear the falls and get a glimpse of them through the rhododendron. The second is for those going on to Le Conte. This is a good place to stop and have lunch. You can climb closer to the falls on huge boulders, but watch for slippery spots.

16. GROTTO FALLS–TRILLIUM GAP TRAIL

Distance: 3 miles (in and out)
Difficulty: Easy
Elevation: Vertical rise is 570 feet in 1.5 miles (3,220 feet to 3,680 feet). Trail presents a steady, gradual climb and an easy return.
How to get there: Trail begins at the Grotto Falls Parking Area. This is about 1.5 miles along the scenic drive known as the Roaring Fork Nature Trail. (A continuation of the Cherokee Orchard Road—see Walk 14. This road is closed in winter. In off-season you can start at the Rainbow Falls trailhead, adding 4 miles to the round-trip hike.)

Grotto Falls is everything its name implies. The ritual is to walk behind the falls, where you have the sensation that you should be wearing a shower cap. It is 1.5 miles to this pleasant spot—a fine short walk through lovely woods along the Trillium Gap Trail (a 6.7-mile trail to Mount Le Conte). Look for dark brown salamanders sunning on rocks in the spray zone below the falls.

The path starts off the Roaring Fork Motor Nature Trail, a very lovely one-way road designed for browsers who wish to get a close look at the flora and fauna without going far from their cars. There are pull-outs for those interested in details, and the whole effect is sylvan and natural. Once you have a taste of the treasures in these woods you will surely want to use your feet for a closer look, out of range of carbon monoxide. In May you should be able to add to your list of wildflowers and check out the wide variety of trees here.

This Grotto Falls portion of the trail is a beginners' walk, so don't worry that it runs along the Roaring Fork, which has the reputation of being the steepest creek along the eastern seaboard. In May the Trillium Gap Trail looks like an immense rustic garden planted with white violets, star chickweed, squawcorn, and Dutchman's breeches. The magnificent trillium also grows profusely and puts one in mind of bevies of demure nuns meditating among the trees. Among the especially fine trees in this old grove are huge hemlocks. Don't be surprised to see a string of eight to ten llamas (and one driver) using this trail to carry food and laundry to Le Conte lodge. Llamas run the supply routes because they do far less trail damage than horses.

We lunched beside the falls in a shaft of sunlight that made its way through the foliage. Early in May the penetration of the sun is possible, but in late spring the density of the leaves would prevent this. The path continues to rise. If you have the time, the woods are pretty enough to warrant continuing farther. Trillium Gap is at 4,700 feet, 1.5 miles beyond the falls. From here a spur trail leads to Brushy Mountain, one of the vantage points from which there is a spectacular view of the Appalachian range. This is only about a half mile and makes the total round-trip from the parking lot a distance of 6.6 miles—a longer trip than we have suggested, but one you might consider.

In wet weather it may be difficult or impossible to cross the creek at Grotto Falls.

Other Walks

(Ask the Park Service for details.)

Appalachian Trail–Boulevard Trail. This is the longest of the five trails to Mount Le Conte, and the beginning portion is described under Newfound Gap–Clingmans Dome walks, where the trail begins. (See Walk 17.)

The high, almost level connecting link between Mount Le Conte and the crest of the Smokies was appropriately named the Boulevard. If you have a reservation for the night at Le Conte Lodge, give this route consideration.

Huskey Gap Trail begins off the Newfound Gap Road about 2 miles south of the Visitor Center and ascends for 2 miles to a gap in Sugarland Mountain. (See Walk 11.)

Boundary Trail, a long trail along the northwest park boundary, starts from behind the park headquarters building. You can stretch your legs for a mile or more on this gently rising path.

Baskins Creek Trail runs 2.7 miles from the Roaring Fork Motor Road just past the Cherokee Orchard into the shaded hardwoods cove along Baskins Creek and passes a pretty waterfall. It climbs out on the far side to join the motor road a few miles from the starting point.

Islands in the Smokies

17. The Jumpoff–Appalachian Trail
18. Appalachian Trail–Road Prong Trail
19. Deep Creek Headwaters
20. Nettle Creek Bald–Thomas Divide Trail
21. Andrews Bald–Forney Ridge Trail
22. Roundtop Knob–Noland Divide Trail

Other Walks: Appalachian Trail, Forney Creek Trail, Sugarland Mountain Trail, Fork Ridge Trail

17. THE JUMPOFF–APPALACHIAN TRAIL

Distance: 6.5 miles (in and out)

Difficulty: Easy to moderate

Elevation: A portion of the Appalachian Trail, vertical rise is 990 feet in 2.7 miles (5,040 feet to 6,030 feet). It presents a steady, gradual climb and an easy return.

How to get there: Trail begins at Newfound Gap, at the northeast edge of the clearing, between the Rockefeller Memorial and the path to the rest rooms.

Newfound Gap is probably the focal point for most people who visit the Smokies—even those who have time only to pass through the park and stop long enough to admire these majestic and mysterious mountains. From the foreground to the horizon, seemingly to infinity, ridge upon misty ridge of densely forested ranges succeed each other. But standing here admiring the view will not provide the close acquaintance this place invites.

The Appalachian Trail is readily accessible from here, and this section has been seriously overused. It comes through Newfound Gap on its way along the ridge of the Smokies. Although it is chiefly a backpacker's paradise, the added day walkers tax the Appalachian Trail severely. When you decide to go on this trail, keep this in mind and choose a time when you might expect less traffic.

Following it eastward offers a moderately easy climb up to the 6,000-foot elevation, a walk through Canadian forest, and good views. Besides the stand of spruce and fir, the only trees at this elevation are the occasional mountain maple, mountain ash, yellow birch, and pin cherry. There are numerous shrubs, ferns, and both spring- and summer-blooming herbs. In 1995, Hurricane Opal blew down many huge trees, mostly within a mile from the start of the trail.

We find the only way to climb is to plug along slowly. On this walk up the slopes of Mount Kephart you gain 300 feet in the first half mile and another 200 feet in the next. When you have gone

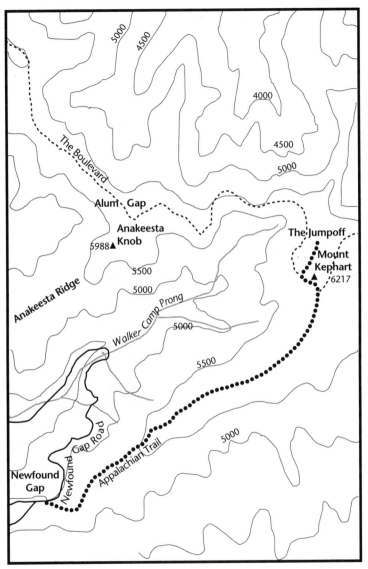

The Jumpoff

1.5 miles, you have climbed nearly 900 feet. (Reaching the 6,030-foot elevation at the Boulevard Trail junction is an easy additional 1.25 miles and will give you a chance to stretch your legs.) Follow the Boulevard Trail left from the junction for a short distance and turn right onto a narrow, rough path at the sign.

Note: The trail from the Boulevard to the Jumpoff is not an official park trail, but its popularity and constant foot traffic keep it open and easy to follow. The environmental impact on the delicate spruce and fir of thousands of boots may dictate that the Park Service abandon this rough track. Check with a ranger or at a visitor Center to ascertain the status of this short spur trail. A plethora of better views exist at Charlies Bunion, as described below.

In approximately a half mile, the path comes out at the Jumpoff, a rocky promontory on the face of Mount Kephart. There are good views from here, including the rocky eminence of Charlies Bunion. This is a nice place to sit and rest before returning. (At the junction you may wish to consider going ahead on the Appalachian Trail to the views from Charlies Bunion, which is 1.5 miles farther along. Just past the junction is Icewater Spring Shelter and a piped spring on the trail.)

There always seems to be something unexpected on these mountain walks, which adds an element of delight to the spirit. In May we saw carpets of the nodding yellow flower of the lily family that has two mottled basal leaves and is known, variously, as trout lily, adder's tongue, or dogtooth violet. We also heard the melodious song of the winter wren.

18. APPALACHIAN TRAIL–ROAD PRONG TRAIL

Distance: From Newfound Gap to Chimney Tops trailhead: 5.0 miles

Difficulty: Moderate to strenuous

Elevation: The 2-mile portion of the Appalachian Trail goes from 5,040 feet almost 500 feet upward, then down to 5,272 feet at Indian Gap. Following the "turnpike" down, elevation drops 1,870

feet in 3.5 miles (5,272 feet to 3,400 feet). If going downhill is difficult for you, this would be strenuous. Many creek crossings make Road Prong Trail difficult in wet weather.

How to get there: Trail begins across the road from the Newfound Gap Parking Area. Look for trail sign and white Appalachian Trail blazes at the western end of a large stone wall.

This walk describes two legs of a triangle and requires hitching a ride back the third leg. You may wish only to go out to Indian Gap and back. We decided it would be interesting to go down the old Indian Gap Road, a toll road built in the 1830s to connect Tennessee and North Carolina—the first wagon road to breach the Smokies. The creek beside the road was named Road Prong, giving the present-day trail its name. Road Prong Trail runs downhill from Indian Gap, dropping 1,870 feet in 3.5 miles. It is therefore rigorous and hard on the knees and legs. We found it exhilarating and recommend it but warn that it is tiring—an instance of downhill being more difficult than uphill.

We parked our car at the Chimneys Parking Area and hitched a ride the short distance up to Newfound Gap. (If you do the two legs, you will be glad to have your car here at the end of the walk.) From the Newfound Gap parking area you must cross the main road to reach the trail. In Walk 17 we mentioned the popularity of the Appalachian Trail especially here as it crosses Newfound Gap. There are apt to be fellow travelers, unless you are out early. It is an exceptionally beautiful part of the trail and is a favorite of wildflower enthusiasts in the spring.

The path dips down a little at first and then climbs gradually through pleasant woods. The undergrowth here is a coarse-textured viburnum known unpoetically as hobblebush. We saw our first rosy twisted-stalk on this path. It is a relative of the Solomon's seal, only the stalk is branched and the little hanging bells are rose colored. There were concentrations of phacelia and trout lilies in mid-May, though they were long gone at the lower altitudes. One of the attractive features of walking the Smokies is this contrast in

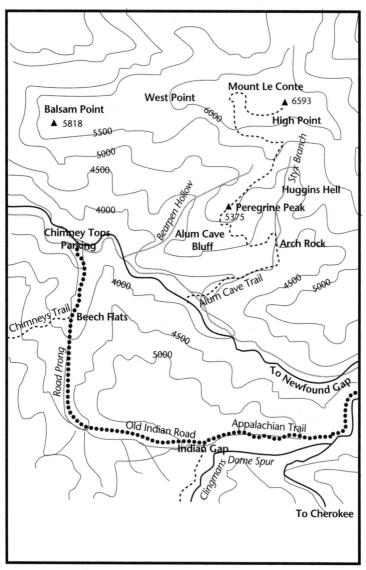

Appalachian Trail–Road Prong Trail

elevations and the resultant changes in life zones that allow you to note these differences.

About a mile from Newfound Gap, the trail goes along a ridge at about 5,400 feet with views to either side. Wire fencing here forms a hog exclosure that protects wildflower bulbs from the rooting of European wild hogs that were introduced accidentally in the 1920s. After another half mile, the trail descends through a dense growth of fir and spruce, somber and still, then comes out to a grassy clearing at Indian Gap on the Clingmans Dome Road.

Road Prong Trail, which leads down to the right, is actually the old Indian Gap Road, only a shadow of its former self. It follows alongside the Road Prong down through the drainage basin. The creek starts as a mere trickle and becomes a roaring, bursting torrent as it gathers velocity on its steep plunge downhill. A side creek washed out in a 1995 flood, piling large trees in the main creek. A trail detour has been routed around the logjam. You can stop and picnic at the first crossing of the creek about a mile down this leg. Here the creek and the path seem to be intertwined, and you may be hopping about on the boulders in the creek quite a bit. As the volume of water increases, the path stays well to the side of the creek. The stands of the unusual umbrella plant are remarkable. You will have a tremendous sense of wilderness, in spite of knowing that the main road is only 2.5 miles below.

We would not have you go unprepared onto this more difficult path, but if you are willing to face it and can take the day doing it, it is one of the finer walks in the Smokies. Check with Park staff about possible hazards at a lower ford of Road Prong if the stream flow is high. Erosion has made the trail very rocky in spots.

19. DEEP CREEK HEADWATERS
Distance: 5 miles (down and back)
Difficulty: Moderate
Elevation: Vertical slope down to the headwaters is 1,480 feet in 2.5 miles (4,680 feet to 3,200 feet). It is a well-graded climb back.

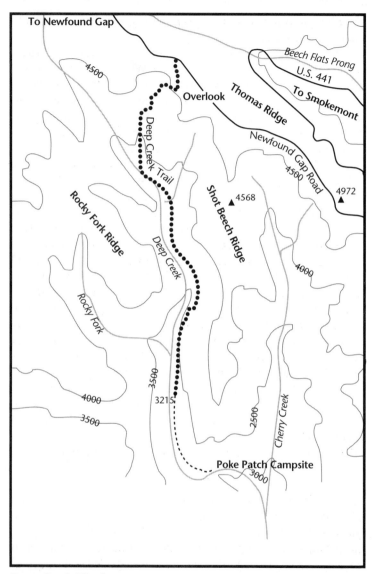

Deep Creek Headwaters

How to get there: Trail begins at a gravel pullout on the New-found Gap Road 1.7 miles south of Newfound Gap. There is a somewhat obscure trail marker on a bank to the right near where the road swings in a curve to the north.

If you are curious about the living wilderness, walking down into the deep ravine where the headwaters of Deep Creek originate may satisfy some of this curiosity. It makes a most interesting and not difficult walk, though there are some soggy places in the trail. A good sturdy pair of boots is advisable. The elevation on the road is 4,800 feet. You drop down to about 3,200 feet in the first mile and a half. After that you can walk another 2 miles without losing much elevation. It is like hiking with a series of switchbacks down into a canyon. The grade is not steep, and if you save the energy for your return climb, you should make it down and back easily.

The general direction is south, but after dropping several hundred feet, the trail works its way northwesterly. It winds with the slopes of the mountainsides as it descends further, then abruptly swings in a hairpin turn at about 1.5 miles and heads south again. While coming down, you hear a noisy little stream off to your left and ford another smaller one. These are tributaries. You will hear Deep Creek coming along before you see it. It will be on your right after 1.5 miles.

At about 2 miles there is considerable moisture as you are almost at the stream level. This is the soggy part of the trail. However, the creek falls away rapidly, and if you continue another half mile, you will be well above the water. You may want to eat your lunch in this area. Should you wish a further objective, you will reach the Poke Patch Campsite at 4 miles.

What makes this walk particularly interesting is the perspective it gives to the steep mountain slope, coves, and deep ravines. Trickling waters form rivulets and run together to make a boisterous, cascading mountain creek. Mature hemlock, maple, beech, and yellow birch inspire awe as you consider their hoary bark and impressive bulk. You sense the impenetrability of wilderness here. It is difficult to imagine roaming through this terrain without a trail to follow. The water is clear and in summer the light is dim. Sunlight is blocked by the high canopy of leaves and penetrates only through those few openings left where one of the giant trees has recently fallen. Here in the valley made by Deep Creek there is mystery filling its shadowy vastness. In April, sunlight flows through the leafless canopy, supporting a carpet of wildflowers, including spring beauty, fringed phacelia, yellow mandarin, and ramps. Black-throated green warblers flit about the open trees and can be spotted when they stop to sing.

20. NETTLE CREEK BALD–THOMAS DIVIDE TRAIL

Distance: 5 miles (in and out)
Difficulty: Easy
Elevation: Vertical rise is 520 feet in 2.5 miles (4,640 feet to 5,160 feet). A gentle grade.
How to get there: Trail begins on the Newfound Gap Road 3 miles south of Newfound Gap.

The Thomas Divide is flanked by the valley of the Oconaluftee River on the east and that of the Deep Creek on the west. The divide is named after "Little Will" Thomas, a white man who was adopted by the Cherokee Indians and later made chief. It vividly illustrates the theory of how the Smokies were carved to their present shapes by erosion. This weathering process, like the forming of the Grand Canyon of Colorado, took millions of years.

As you enter the woods, you begin to go gradually downhill almost immediately. This continues for about .25 mile, and then you climb slowly along the narrow spine of Beetree Ridge for the next half mile. In front of a great hulk of a fallen tree, the trail makes an abrupt hairpin turn to the left. It continues gradually climbing to the crest of the ridge at 5,160 feet, a distance from the start of about 1.25 miles. Here there is an opening alongside a giant oak tree with a fine view straight ahead to the crest of the Smokies—Mount Kephart, Charlies Bunion, and the lower ridge of

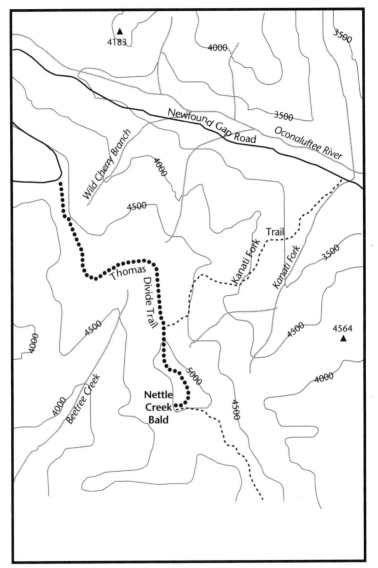

Nettle Creek Bald

Richland Mountain in the foreground. To the southeast there is a view of the Balsams.

The trail stays at about this elevation for another 1.25 miles. It leads to the Nettle Creek Bald, which appears from the trail as only a tunnel through a rhododendron patch. This is a good turn-around. (The National Park Service sign for the Kanati Fork Trail comes before Nettle Creek Bald at 1.8 miles, leading off to your left back down to the Newfound Gap Road in 3 miles—a descent of just over 2,000 feet. It could make a good alternate route or extension to your walk if you can arrange transportation back to your car. Kanati Fork supports masses of creekside wildflowers in spring.)

Elevation is one of the principal factors determining life zones. This walk floats along on the 5,000-foot level for nearly 3 miles, passing through stands of very large oaks and maples, with a few hemlocks and a great variety of herblike plants. Wildflowers abound. Columbine, Canada mayflower, pink lady's-slipper and quantities of white clintonia (venturing a little above its usual elevation) bloom here in the spring. Rotting American chestnut logs lie scattered along the ridgetop. Gently lift small slabs of wood beside the trail to check for red-cheeked salamanders or giant millipedes. Turk's cap lily, wild bergamot, and dodder bloom in summer.

It is easy to walk rhythmically here. Covering distance is quite painless, and a steady pace is not hard to maintain. Because of this you may wish to stretch your legs still more. The trail is 14 miles to Deep Creek Campground, so you ought to be able to get as much exercise as you want.

21. ANDREWS BALD–FORNEY RIDGE TRAIL

Distance: 3.6 miles (down and back)
Difficulty: Moderate
Elevation: Vertical fall is 500 feet in 1.8 miles (6,300 feet to 5,800 feet). The slope down into the meadow is an easy but rocky walk, requiring close attention to the path. Coming back is a steady climb.

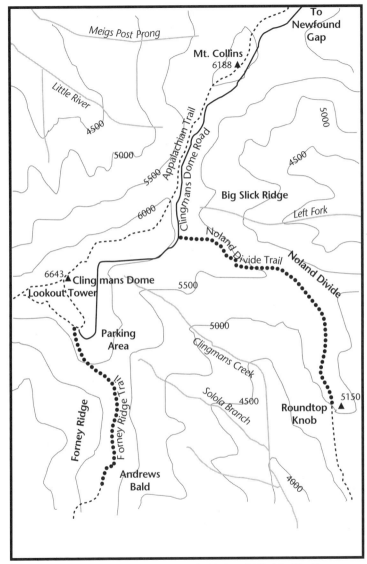

Andrews Bald and Roundtop Knob–Noland Divide Trail

How to get there: Trail begins at the Forney Ridge Parking Area near Clingmans Dome. The road from Newfound Gap to Clingmans Dome is closed November to April.

The Park Service features Andrews Bald in organized walks and literature, so you are apt to hear about it. It is also more accessible than the other balds. Do not let this deter you, for it is a beautiful high-country walk with its own special flavor.

The trail leaves the west end of the Clingmans Dome Parking Area and goes out over Forney Ridge. It runs downhill for the first mile, then across a fairly level saddle and uphill again to the bald. The spruce and fir forest characteristics that you find at this 6,300-foot elevation disappear completely. Suddenly you come upon a whole hilltop of grassy expanse. It is a delightful trip to make into a day's outing. Andrews Bald is a perfect picnic spot, open to the sun with glorious views of the towering ranges in the national forest of North Carolina and Georgia.

The walk itself is full of interest, and because it is rough and rocky, it is a good one to take slow and easy. As the crowds gravitate toward Clingmans Dome, you turn left into a dark spruce and fir forest with immense rock outcroppings that dwarf everything. The voices of those walking up to Clingmans Dome Tower grow dimmer and dimmer. Trees grow very close together and let in little light. The forest floor is strewn with a haphazard mixture of downed tree hulks and gigantic boulders. The only plants that seem to thrive in this dark forest are mosses, ferns, and the bluebead lily (clintonia, which grows to 18 inches tall). However, a combination of air pollution and an introduced insect is killing the fir trees, so you may see more skeletal dead trees here than live ones.

The path goes steadily along the rocks. After a half mile or so it comes out of the woods and onto a ridge with small clusters of cherry trees and blueberry bushes. You can see off to the south. You go on for a while and then into more woods, past the junction where the Forney Creek Trail goes right. You go along the saddle into the open again at the bald.

We saw deer tracks all the way out, so we suppose the deer graze on the grasses of Andrews Bald. It is said that these balds, which are found throughout the Smokies, were caused by lightning fires and subsequently kept open by cattle driven up to higher elevations in the summer. Andrews Bald and Gregory Bald are now being maintained by the Park Service, and the other high Smokies balds are becoming overgrown with trees. Rhododendron and flame azalea make a colorful showing here toward the end of June. In July and August, raspberries and blackberries ripen, and in September there are plenty of high bush blueberries for bears, birds, and hikers. Whatever the season, it is worth the trip.

An interesting sidelight is the way the name of Andrews Bald itself was changed when written. Originally this was an area used for grazing by a family down in the valley whose name was Anders. Old timers are said to still call it "Anders Bald."

22. ROUNDTOP KNOB–NOLAND DIVIDE TRAIL

Distance: 4 miles (down and back)

Difficulty: Easy to moderate

Elevation: Vertical fall is 729 feet in 2 miles (5,929 feet to 5,200 feet). The slope down to the knob is an easy walk. Coming back is a steady, graded climb.

How to get there: Trail begins on the Clingmans Dome Road , 5.5 miles from Newfound Gap, 0.25 mile beyond the Thomas Ridge Overlook, and 1.5 miles back from the Clingmans Dome Parking Area.

The several life zones within the Great Smoky Mountains National Park add much interest to walking here, for it is possible to see an especially wide range of plants and animals. Some of the flora occur at different elevations and hence will mature at different times. If you miss the trillium down below, you may catch it later if you take a walk at a higher elevation.

This easily accessible walk along the spine of the Noland Divide is mostly through Canadian-zone vegetation. Because of its elevation, it receives approximately 80 inches of rainfall annually. The trees, notably yellow birch, are unusually large.

You start out at the gated road off the Clingmans Dome Road, 0.25 mile beyond the Webb Overlook. Park your car by the gate and walk down the road 0.5 mile where it comes to an acid deposition study tower. Here you will find the trail that takes off left along the "divide," Smoky parlance for a ridge that runs at right angles to its main east-west rim. It is possible to walk about 6 miles out on this divide before it starts a deep descent. Although you move to a lower elevation, you may not notice because it is so gradual, or perhaps it is because the walk is so pleasant that you are not aware of how much elevation you are losing. There are subtle changes in vegetation as the Fraser fir is replaced by oak and beech, the yellow clintonia lily by the white.

We only went 2 miles, to a laurel slick called Roundtop Knob, a rocky area where shallow-rooted laurel can grow. It is a good turn-around because when you start back, your legs have to pump harder. The Smokies have many of these slicks punctuating their otherwise dark-green flanks. In the spring when they are pink with blossoms, they light up the somber hills in wide patches.

This is an especially silent path, spongy and resilient underfoot, away from road sounds and without the usual babbling brook. We had not gone far when the song we often heard at these elevations penetrated the silence. The tiny winter wren seemed close at hand.

It began to rain while we were on the divide. Coming back we got a clear picture of how erosion works—even on woodland paths. The spongy path we had walked on had lost its absorbency and filled up.

Other Walks
(Ask the Park Service for details.)

From Clingmans Dome west on the **Appalachian Trail** it is 4.1 miles to Silers Bald, a descent of 1,200 feet. East on the Appalachian Trail to the summit of Mount Collins is 3 miles (453 feet lower).

Forney Creek Trail cuts right from the Forney Ridge Trail 1 mile (see Walk 21) from the parking area and drops rapidly to the creek in 1.8 miles, a descent to about 4,000 feet from the 6,300 feet at the parking area. Its descent is along old railroad beds through a mixed spruce and hardwood forest.

Sugarland Mountain Trail ends on the Appalachian Trail near Mount Collins, having come almost 12 miles from the Little River Road. If you walk out on it, there are great views of Mount Le Conte and Mount Mingus. The beginning of the trail is on Clingmans Dome Road 4.5 miles west of Newfound Gap. Just opposite the Fork Ridge Trail, hike west (left) about 0.5 mile on the Appalachian Trail to the Sugarland Mountain Trail.

Fork Ridge Trail runs about 5 miles to the Poke Patch Campsite on Deep Creek. It follows along the crest of the ridge for just under 4 miles, through an old growth forest of fir and spruce with massive boulders and many ferns and wildflowers.

Greenbrier–Cosby Area

23. Albright Grove–Maddron Bald Trail
24. Ramsay Cascades
25. Porters Creek
26. Henwallow Falls–Gabes Mountain Trail
27. Sutton Ridge–Lower Mount Cammerer Trail
Other Walks: Brushy Mountain Trail, Cosby Nature Trail, Low Gap Trail, Snake Den Ridge Trail

Ramsay Cascades

23. ALBRIGHT GROVE–MADDRON BALD TRAIL

Distance: 7 miles (up and back)

Difficulty: Moderate

Elevation: Vertical rise is 1,500 feet in 3.5 miles (1,880 feet to 3,380 feet). Trail presents a steady, gentle grade but is not easy because the total distance must be accounted for. Returning, however, is not difficult.

How to get there: One must be on the alert to find the beginning of this trail. It is about 16 miles east from Gatlinburg on U.S. 321. About 1 mile past the Yogi Bear Jellystone Camp-Resort on the south side of the road is narrow, gravel Laurel Springs Road, which runs along the park boundary. Turn south onto it and in 1.3 miles, the gated entrance to the trail will appear on your left. (The trail marker says MADDRON BALD TRAIL.) Parking is tight, and Laurel Springs Road is rocky and eroded.

It's a rather long walk and an uphill climb, but the goal is so spectacular you will never regret the effort. Being in the Albright Grove has the kind of effect that lingers in your memory for instant recall, soothes the spirit with profound quiet, gives nourishment to the soul. You will ponder the fabulous size of these ancient yellow poplars and may see one that is thought to be the oldest living thing in the East. The grove is awesome and unique. It was named after Horace Albright, the distinguished second director of the National Park Service and one of the principals in the development of these Smokies as a national park.

The service road is closed to cars, and it looks, amidst a lovely cover of rhododendron, like an entrance to someone's private estate. This is the start of Maddron Bald Trail, which leads you in 1.2 miles to Gabes Mountain Trail and in 2 miles farther to the grove. (This is mentioned on the trail sign.)

The uphill climb is not so steep as to be fatiguing but is good for setting a pace and keeping with it. At 0.5 mile there is an unusual cabin, the only one of its kind remaining in the park. It was built by the Willis Baxters, who farmed this land. According

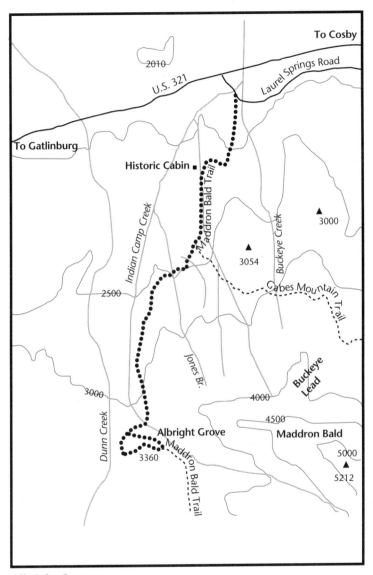

Albright Grove

to Ed Trout, park historian, it was constructed from one giant chestnut. The trunk was split again and again into slabs 2 to 4 inches thick and 8 to 12 inches wide, which form the walls.

It was known as a weaner, or honeymoon cabin. The Baxter homestead was across the road, and when a child married, the new couple lived in the cabin until they built their own home.

Shortly after you pass the cabin, the road crosses Cole Creek and starts running alongside it. Looking down, there are white-water vistas through the fairly sparse growth of trees on this former farmland. The Gabes Mountain Trail comes in on the left shortly after 1 mile, and at 2.3 miles the service road comes to a turnaround. It is here, on the south side, that the Maddron Bald Trail, which takes you to the grove, begins.

In spring this path is lined with white violets and strewn with mountain silverbells. If you see these surroundings with a little low-lying fog, common in the Smokies, it is especially beautiful. The trail crosses Indian Camp Creek on a footlog slab. We were enchanted by the waterfall here, with the artistic way the huge boulders shape these waters into a series of fountains.

From this bridge the path goes sharply up the side of the ravine. After about 0.75 mile, the Albright Grove Nature Trail goes straight ahead, while the Maddron Bald Trail keeps left. The nature trail goes through the ancient trees and comes out again on the Maddron Bald Trail 0.7 mile from the point you left it. Turn left and you are headed back. Giant tulip poplars, beeches, silverbells, hemlocks, and Fraser magnolias show what much of the park looked like before logging.

At our pace it took us about an hour and a half to come up. We spent an hour in the grove, and the return to our car took another hour. We listened to the mellow sounds of the thrush and the splashing of the brook overlaying the marvelous solitude. A break in the clouds allowed sunlight to filter through and put a sparkle on the wet rhododendron leaves. As we left the park, we took fresh trout with us from a nearby trout farm, where they obligingly dressed two beauties.

24. RAMSAY CASCADES

Distance: 8 miles (up and back)

Difficulty: Strenuous

Elevation: Vertical rise is 2,250 feet in 4 miles (2,150 feet to 4,400 feet). Trail presents a steady, gradual climb and an easier return.

How to get there: By car the trailhead is 4.5 miles from U.S. 321 on the Greenbrier Road (6 miles east of Gatlinburg). The driving will be slow because the road is narrow. After about 3 miles (shortly after the picnic area), the road forks. There will be a sign; turn to the left, across the bridge over the Middle Prong of the Little Pigeon River. Here the road narrows, climbs, crosses five bridges and continues 1.5 miles—at which point there is ample parking on both sides of the road.

One of the publicized walks in the Smokies is this pathway upstream alongside the tumbling Ramsay Prong of the Little Pigeon River. It is considered strenuous because of the steady climb and the distance to Ramsay Cascades. Despite this, it is a popular walk to one of the largest waterfalls in the park.

The trail crosses the river and immediately begins to climb on an old road. In 1.5 miles it gains over 500 feet. A brook, Ramsay Branch, pours from your left under the path into the river on your right. The road then becomes a footpath, and you meet the Ramsay Prong and continue to follow it upstream to the cascades.

We made it up to the cascades from the gate in just three and a half hours—a slow pace, but this trail offers many distractions. Others puffed their way around us while we crossed the three log bridges and walked across the streams on rocks. We took it gradually, stopping to inspect wildflowers blooming, the bark of ancient trees, and a snail moving slowly on a rotting log. Innumerable other tiny natural phenomena occupied us and slowed our pace.

When we arrived hours later at the cascades, we were met by a large group numbering fifteen or more. Another man, seeing them, said to us, "This isn't exactly my idea of a wilderness experience!" If you come here expecting to be alone, you are apt to

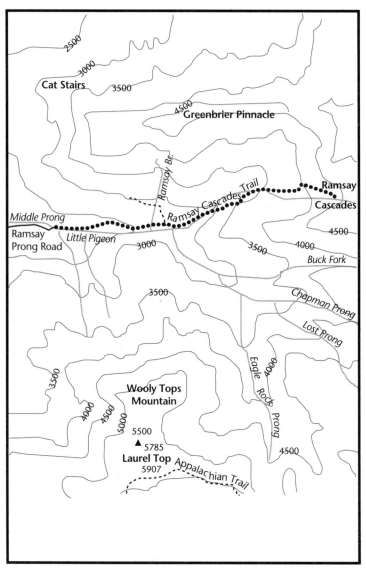

Ramsay Cascades

express a similar fleeting disappointment. The experience, however, is impressive. On either side of the trail, growth is rampant. It runs up the steep slopes unchecked except by age or disaster. Nearly everything is covered with moss or lichen. Rotting hulks of enormous trees lie fallen at capricious angles. One scarcely notices the lacy, young pale-green ferns, but they act as a garnish throughout. The overwhelming size and numbers of trees and the variety of growing forms of life are, after all, essential ingredients in the "wilderness experience." At the falls, several huge boulders provide the only sunny spots of the hike. Here you can eat lunch, soak your feet, and admire the 90-foot cascade.

The ancient trees of this area are a real rarity. In this cove many of them show the ravages of time. Despite deformities, they are magnificent. Several between the first and second log bridges are among the largest specimens in the park. Look through your tree guide before you start, and be prepared to explore the path for eastern hemlock, mountain silverbell, black birch, cucumber tree (of the magnolia family), black cherry, and the "tulip tree" or yellow poplar. You will see birch trees that are standing up on their roots like ballet dancers. They had grown originally on fallen trunks of other trees. When the trunks disintegrated, they were left poised in midair—a curious sight.

25. PORTERS CREEK

Distance: 3.5 miles (in and out)
Difficulty: Easy
Elevation: Vertical rise is 650 feet in 1.75 miles (1,900 feet to 2,550 feet). Trail is on a gentle grade. Coming back is a breeze.
How to get there: Trail begins at the end of the Porters Creek Road. Follow Greenbrier Road from U.S. 321 (as in Walk 24) to the fork at the bridge, but go straight on for another mile to the parking area and turnaround. Greenbrier Road is rough from flood damage, and large vehicles such as campers are not allowed.

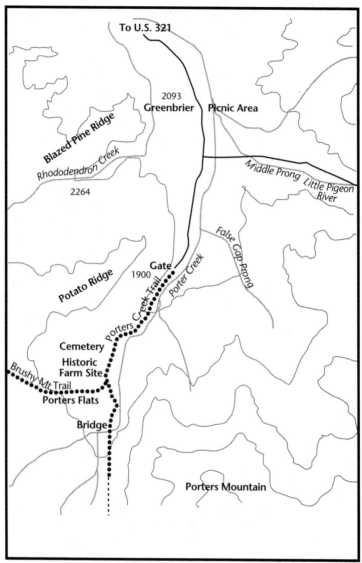

Porters Creek

There was once a primitive campsite in Greenbrier Cove, but it has now been converted to a picnic area. The park maintains no development here other than the trails, so people looking for quiet and wilderness should not overlook this area.

Porters Creek flows north out of the mountains to join the Little Pigeon River. The trail along Porters Creek is a beauty—less traveled and softer underfoot than Ramsay Cascade Trail. It is a gravel road for the first mile and the deep cool woods it goes through are ideal for a family outing.

The road is graded, and on the right at about .75 mile from the starting gate, you will find old homesites and a cemetery. Many of the graves are marked in the mountain fashion with headstones and footstones, though few are identified with names. At approximately 1 mile, the road splits for a short distance to form a loop. You will see flat land that would be good for farming, but you will have to imagine it as it once was—a clear and fertile valley. It is now grown over with timber.

At the right fork is a sign: HISTORIC FARM SITE—200 YARDS. This path is well worth taking to John Messer's cantilevered barn (1875) and spring house and the former Smoky Mountain Hiking Club Cabin. The cabin was built between 1934 and 1936 with logs from old cabins and is now owned and preserved by the park.

At the top of the road loop, on the right, is a trail sign to Brushy Mountain and Mount Le Conte. Trillium Gap is 4.3 miles up this trail.

Our path is on the left fork and leaves the road on a trail along Porters Creek. Painted trillium grows on the mossy tops of boulders.

After about a half mile of pleasant walking, a beautiful tree-trunk bridge spans the creek. Here you get a view up and down the immense boulder-strewn bed that diverts the water and makes the valley resound with its energy. About half a mile beyond the bridge up on the slope is the long, narrow Fern Branch Falls we've suggested as a turnaround. The area between the bridge and the falls is well-known as one of the best wildflower walks in the park; on spring weekends, trailhead parking can be a problem.

The trail continues beyond for 2 miles to end at campsite No. 31. Many walkers may wish to continue. The footing is fair and if you have the time and stamina, walk on for a while. The trail provides a classic setting—large hardwood trees; water cascading down from several streams; and fallen trunks, now moss-covered relics of the past. The gap between the path and the creek is filled with rhododendron. Fresh prints in the soft earth told us deer were here. We strolled along a mile or so, seeing furry white flowers of the spring season, particularly noticeable in this deep forest—the false spikenard, foam flower, clintonia, phacelia, baneberry, false Solomon's seal, and bishop's cap. (With guide books these are much easier to spot.)

The cliche of "cathedral-like atmosphere" comes to mind here because the path is so soft and silent and the tall trees Gothic in proportion. We spotted rose-breasted grosbeak in mountain silverbells and our first black-throated blue warbler of the spring season. Coming back was all downhill. We kept a steady pace, making the return in much less time. We passed a trout fisherman in the stream and saw a scarlet tanager and a vireo in our glasses. You might do even better and see that deer.

26. HENWALLOW FALLS–GABES MOUNTAIN TRAIL

Distance: 4.4 miles (up and back)
Difficulty: Easy to moderate
Elevation: Vertical rise is 640 feet in 2.2 miles (2,240 feet to 2,880 feet). Trail presents an easy-graded climb for 1 mile and levels out to the falls. An easy return.
How to get there: Trail begins opposite the entrance to the Cosby Picnic Area; look for Gabes Mountain Trail sign.

It was a fine clear day the last of April when we walked to Henwallow Falls, but the density of the woods was only occasionally punctured by sunlight. We were able to find a cluster of trailing arbutus still in blossom and enjoy its delicate fragrance. The walk from Cosby Picnic Area and the return are easy and pleasant.

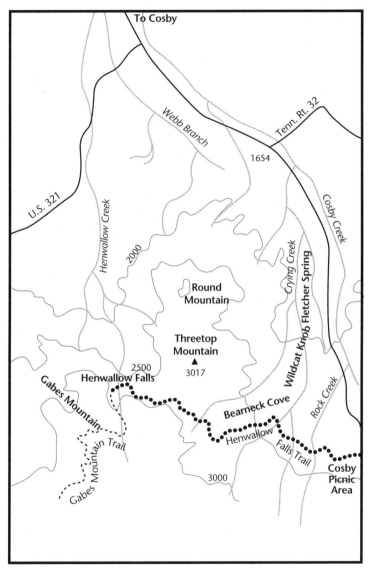

Henwallow Falls–Gabes Mountain Trail

It took us between two and two and a half hours.

The words *delicate* and *mysterious* best describe the impression these woods made on us. It was one unexpected excitement after another—giant hemlock and yellow poplar, gorgeous pink lady's-slipper and white clintonia almost ready to bloom, and squawroot in great clumps under the oaks. Henwallow Falls are delicate cascades. The water spills and splashes over eighteen or more levels and spreads over a large, flat rock surface into a thin sheet of white foam.

The trail moves through mixed, second-growth hardwoods for some distance, then crosses Rock Creek on one of four bridges, each made of the trunk of a large tree as much as 40 feet long. It next enters a grove principally of eastern hemlock with delicate foliage. After crossing through a small stand of holly and across Crying Creek on the last of the bridges, you will have come three-quarters of a mile. Here the trail starts a long gradual climb over the next half mile until it reaches a break known as Messer Gap. From here a short path leads up a little knoll to a grave.

The last half mile levels out (more or less) and winds along the contour of Gabes Mountain, along large outcroppings of rock. The trail has been shelved out all along for an easy pathway. Very shortly you reach the signed cutoff descending to the falls on the right. Before or after you visit the falls, you will want to continue on the main trail westward a very short distance to a clearing. There is a bench here and a good view of the valley of Cosby Creek and Big Ridge on the other side. Just 100 yards beyond this is Henwallow Creek. You will be amazed to see how small a creek can produce such an impressive cascade.

27. SUTTON RIDGE–LOWER MOUNT CAMMERER TRAIL

Distance: 3 miles (out and back)

Difficulty: Easy

Elevation: Vertical rise is 370 feet in 1.5 miles (2,320 feet to 2,690 feet). Trail climbs about 100 feet within 0.75 mile, then gains

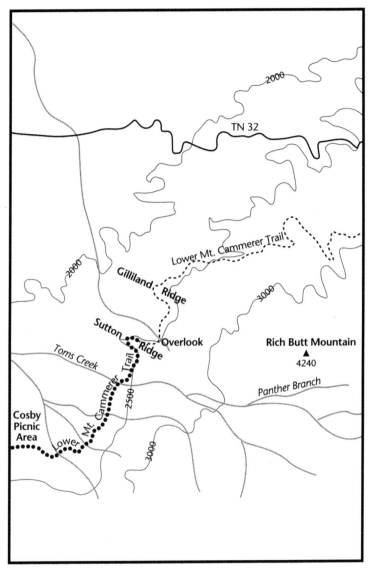

2000

TN 32

2000

Lower Mt. Cammerer Trail

Gilliland Ridge

3000

Sutton Ridge

Overlook

Rich Butt Mountain
▲
4240

Toms Creek

Mt. Cammerer Trail

2500

Panther Branch

Cosby
Picnic
Area

Lower

3000

Sutton Ridge–Lower Mount Cammerer Trail

another 100 feet over a mile and finally presents a short, steep climb to the lookout. Return walk is all downhill.

How to get there: Trail begins at the upper east side of Cosby Campground, near the amphitheater. Continue straight ahead on the paved road and turn left at the gated road, which is marked.

For a fine, easy-to-reach view of the rim of the Appalachians, Cosby Knob, Inadu Knob, Maddron Bald, and the Cosby Valley, be sure to take this short walk up to Sutton Ridge. It begins right at the Cosby Campground and does not take very long. The trail is 1.5 miles in length and is gently rolling most of the way.

You cross Cosby Creek on the bridge and stay right on this old road. Again, quite soon, it crosses another brook. Along this first part of the trail through hemlock and hardwoods, beautiful wildflowers are everywhere. At about half a mile this road swings left and the trail bears right through a rhododendron patch and on to Sutton Ridge.

There is virtually no climbing along this trail, except for a short scramble up to Sutton Ridge. It winds and curves along the contour of the side of Mount Cammerer with a slight rise or fall. At a mile and a half another sign points to a switchback trail that leads to the clearing. We sat here quite a while and admired the lovely views from the ridge. The wind swept into the grove of pine and buckeye here on the ridge. The humidity, which had been so oppressive from a morning rain, was gone. Puddles you might expect after such a rain had been absorbed by the humus of the forest floor. Even the fallen, dried leaves showed no sogginess. In the few days we had been in the park, the foliage had come out. Banks that had been carpeted with iris a few weeks ago now had only a stray, faded blossom remaining. Shortly the laurel would be in bloom. Observations like these at any time of year are inevitable, for nature provides a wonderful world of rapid changes.

Our walk here was not quite long enough, so we went along the path another mile or so through a piney woods where the footing is cushiony. The trail crosses several small mountain streams, one of which falls 75 feet or so over perfectly terraced rock formations. The humid woods were full of orchis and trillium, especially toadshade. We saw a patch of velvety, maroon wakerobin, and the dainty puttyroot. The steep ravines were filled with rhododendron. Coming back to Cosby we spied a rosebud—one lone, pink rose—still blooming. Nature changes rapidly, and you may not see this bloom or feel the wind as we did, but if you are observant, you will find your own enjoyment.

Other Walks
(Ask the Park Service for details.)

Brushy Mountain Trail starts near the Porters Creek Trail (see Walk 21) and is 4.5 miles to Trillium Gap, a strenuous climb of 2,800 feet. For a shorter day hike in wild country, you can climb 1,550 feet in 3.3 miles to a view of Mount Le Conte and another 300 feet into a grove of large poplars and hemlock at 3.7 miles.

The self-guided **Cosby Nature Trail** is at Cosby Campground by the amphitheater. Nearly level, it runs beside a small creek and has beautiful spring wildflowers.

Low Gap Trail leads from the campground up to the Appalachian Trail over a former service road to Low Gap, a steep climb of 1,950 feet in 2.5 miles. Mount Cammerer, with a rebuilt fire tower and 360° views, is 2.7 miles farther from Low Gap on the Appalachian Trail.

Snake Den Ridge Trail out of Cosby Campground is a climb of 1,100 feet in 2 miles to Inadu Creek through large buckeye, poplar, locust, and hemlock woods. To continue from here is a steep climb, but there are occasional peek-through views. By 4.5 miles the trail has climbed 3,000 feet to reach the side trail to nearby Maddron Bald. Snake Den Ridge Trail meets the Appalachian Trail in 0.7 mile more.

Cherokee Area

Hardwood Forest

28. KEPHART PRONG

Distance: 4 miles (up and back)
Difficulty: Easy
Elevation: Vertical rise is 830 feet in 2 miles (2,730 feet to 3,560 feet). Trail presents a steady, graded climb.
How to get there: Trail begins 3.7 miles north of Smokemont Campground on Newfound Gap Road.

The prong is an irrepressible surge of water that empties into the Oconaluftee River near its source. It bubbles its way in, out, and around huge boulders, pours over rills, and skips around the rocky edges. As you leave the parking area on the Newfound Gap Road, the woods have a heavy understory of rhododendron and are dense and dark. They soon lighten and become much thinner and more open. Spring wildflowers of many varieties abound. We were pleased to find the putty root, an orchid with yellow-green flowers. Its root, when pounded, makes a mucilaginous substance that pioneer women used to mend pottery.

When we started this walk, the sky looked threatening. It cleared up later in the day, as it often does. Rain, as you quickly find out, is something you can be sure of in the Smokies. You should always be prepared and carry some raingear with you.

The trail first crosses a bridge over the Oconaluftee River, then comes to an abandoned camp, which during the 1930s was a Civilian Conservation Corps camp. You will see traces of it—a signpost, a rock chimney, and the kind of planting seen in inhabited areas, including spreading juniper and boxwood. To the left is an old cement cistern that supplied water to a trout-raising operation.

At .25 mile the old road turns left to ford the stream, which you need not do. The trail continues straight on and turns left sharply to cross on a sturdy bridge and rejoin the road on the other side. The road you follow fords the prong four times. Walkers are provided bridges and footlogs not exactly where the road fords, but nearby. You will see the signs. Do not rush across these, because each is a delight to the eyes. The old road becomes rocky

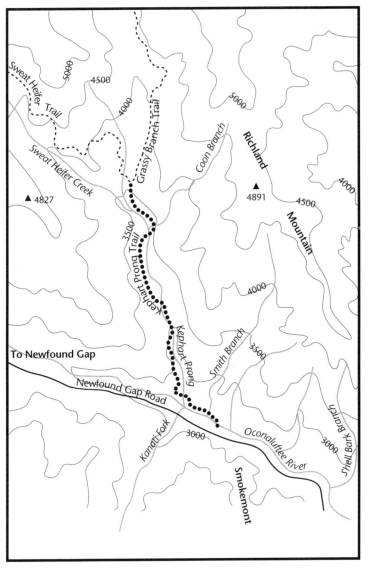

Kephart Prong

in spots, but still presents an easy rise. When you come to the National Park Service shelter, you have come 2 miles and climbed almost a thousand feet. This can be your turnaround. If you wish to extend your walk, you can try one of the two trails that start here at the shelter.

The Grassy Branch Trail leads off to the right and up to the ridge of Richland Mountain, the hulk that parallels the Newfound Gap Road to the east. It is a climb of 1,740 feet in 2.5 miles and does not break out into a view until you reach the top.

The Sweat Heifer Trail goes on up to the Appalachian Trail, climbing 2,270 feet in 3.5 miles. You have to cross the stream on the footbridge in front of the shelter to reach this trail. The trail ascends gradually, following an old railroad bed and crossing many small creeks on stepping stones. It seemed a gay and cheerful place to us after coming through all the rhododendron. Here the chief undergrowth is fern and partridgeberry. The mountain the trail climbs is Mount Kephart, named for Horace Kephart, an early advocate of the park and author of *Our Southern Highlanders,* about the people of the Smokies.

29. SMOKEMONT LOOP

Distance: 6 miles
Difficulty: Moderate
Elevation: Vertical rise is 1,260 feet in 3 miles (2,220 feet to 3,480 feet). Trail is graded about the same up and down.
How to get there: Trail begins at the parking area near the gate at the end of the Smokemont Campground.

You won't find a more pleasant woodland walk than the Smokemont Loop. Ascribing special qualities to certain walks is not scientific, because seasonal variations, weather conditions, and personal preferences must be taken into consideration. There is something almost continually of interest close to the trail. After you have reached the ridge, there are peek-through views east and west.

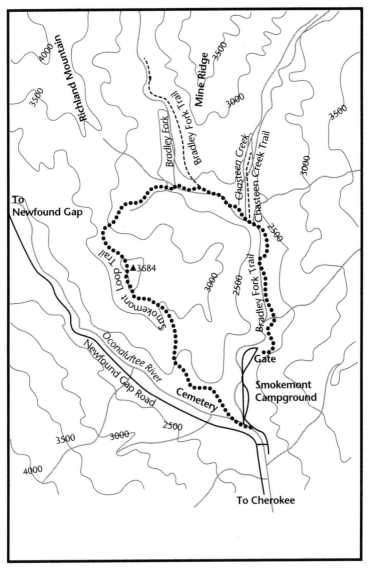

Smokemont Loop

You park your car at the gated road at the upper end of Smokemont Campground. The first 1.7 miles are straight ahead along Bradley Fork Trail, through large groves of rhododendron and fine stands of maidenhair fern. There are three clearings with plants left over from the days when people lived here—boxwood, syringa, roses, and plum trees. Some birds, like the indigo bunting, set up their territories in open places like these.

At 1.7 miles the loop trail leaves the Bradley Fork Trail and crosses Bradley Fork on a very low, narrow log bridge and then turns left. This 3.9-mile path is soft with leafmold in the area along the stream. You will discover it is quiet, for you have turned away from the creek, and the forest muffles its sound. The creek plain and hillside abound with spring flowers: phlox, trillium, jack-in-the-pulpit, Clinton's lily, and more. The trail climbs the eastern slopes of Richland Mountain, crossing over its ridge at 3 miles. There is a National Park Service sign and a flourishing stand of pink lady's-slipper. The trail continues southward to a higher elevation of 3,460 feet before descending and recrossing the creek into the campground.

Although completely cut over, this second-growth woods has taken hold extremely well because of heavy natural rainfall and a sheltered location. It displays a wide variety of wildflowers, trees, and shrubs. Anyone interested in the woods should find it a rewarding walk with easy grades and fitting surroundings in which to spend a leisurely four to five hours.

As it winds down the southern slope of the mountain, the path goes through a deep cove where the gaunt hulks of ancient chestnut logs are strewn on the floor. Although you may feel you are in a graveyard of giants, look again and see the many seedlings that are beginning to spring up—leaves of poplar, maple, red, scarlet, and white oak only a few inches above the ground. They are an example of the forest renewing itself naturally.

The trail drops to a service road through a marshy area and passes Bradley Cemetery. You return by crossing Bradley Fork on a concrete bridge at the lower edge of the campground. The loop is completed by a half-mile walk through the campground to the parking area.

30. MINGUS MILL ROAD

Distance: 4 miles (in and out)
Difficulty: Easy
Elevation: Vertical rise is 730 feet in 2 miles (2,050 feet to 2,780 feet). Trail is well graded.
How to get there: Trail begins from the parking lot by the Mingus Mill on the Newfound Gap Road north of Cherokee.

We suggest you visit the Pioneer Farmstead alongside the Oconaluftee Visitor Center before you take this walk. This will give you a perspective for contemplation. Having seen this living exhibit, go on to the Mingus Mill, a half mile north on the Newfound Gap Road. You will be able to watch the corn being ground between the enormous stones and see the ingenuity of the mill race, the sluice, and the water-turned steel turbine.

The Great Smoky Mountains Natural History Association has assisted the National Park Service in preserving these features of pioneer days. They are beautifully and simply conceived and set one to pondering the different values held by our forebears and the contrast with what life has become today.

The Mingus Mill Road goes off on a gated service road. Walk up the creek on the road beginning from the parking lot side. It is a gravel road, crossing the creek three times on bridges. You will see that there were dwellings along it, for it comes into clearings every now and again where a rosebush or two still bloom on land that was privately owned more than sixty years ago.

As you go along, you will see a firing range to the right where the rangers practice. The woods are mostly hardwoods here with an understory of rhododendron and many wildflowers in spring. At 1 mile the trail comes upon a water supply treatment area, sitting in a field of wild strawberries. At this point the service road

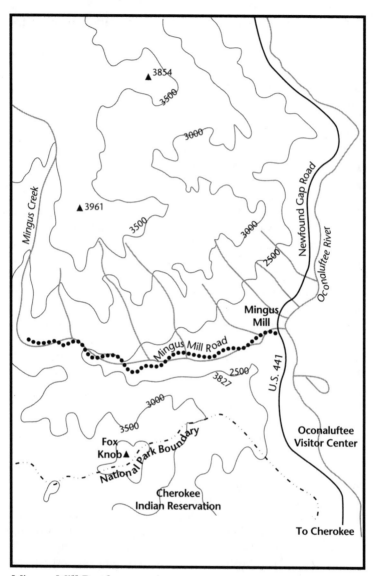

Mingus Mill Road

peters out. At 1.2 miles the road forks, having passed Madcap Branch where it enters Mingus Creek. The Mingus Creek Trail, which starts at the end of Mingus Mill Road, climbs on up to Newton Bald via Madcap Branch.

We were advised to take, and we recommend that you take, the right-hand fork that follows Mingus Creek. It is a pretty trail and leads eventually to some very large rocks on the right at about 1.7 miles from this junction. You will find a path through these rocks leading up a short distance to an old cemetery, which ties in with the pioneer beginnings we described.

31. RAVEN FORK–HYATT RIDGE AND ENLOE CREEK TRAILS

Distance: 6 miles (in and out)

Difficulty: Strenuous

Elevation: In 3 miles the trail goes up 1,490 feet (2,935 feet to 4,425 feet) and down 805 feet (4,425 feet to 3,620 feet) to the bridge. The return has a climb of 805 feet and then down.

How to get there: Trail begins from a parking area on the Round Bottom Road, about 13.5 miles from the Oconaluftee Visitor Center. To reach the parking area, drive southeast from the visitor center about 1.5 miles to Big Cove Road and turn left. Then, after crossing the river, turn left again at the stop sign. Follow Big Cove Road through the Cherokee Reservation till it forks. Take the right fork (it shortly becomes a gravel road) to a parking area on the left, about 2.5 miles beyond the gate at the park boundary. There is a sign for Hyatt Ridge Trail. The Enloe Creek Trail starts 1.9 miles from the parking area.

Note: The gate at the park boundary is closed in the winter, thus adding 2.5 miles hiking distance.

We certainly would not recommend this walk to everyone. It is a strenuous climb of 1,500 feet on Hyatt Ridge Trail from the Round Bottom Road up to the beginning of Enloe Creek Trail. It is

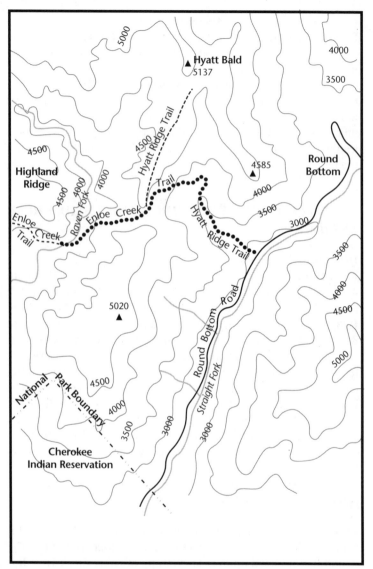

Raven Fork–Hyatt Ridge and Enloe Creek Trails

relentlessly uphill all the way on an old road heavily used by horses and consequently rutted and muddy in some spots. However, it runs beside a pretty creek with jack-in-the-pulpit, Clinton's lily, fire pink, and many other flowers on its banks.

After this 2-mile walk uphill through second-growth woods, you come to a junction. You then must go 1 more mile down on the Enloe Creek Trail, a steep trail that drops 800 feet to the bridge and hence must be climbed on your return. This mile down is also a well-used horse trail, which continues on westward climbing up Hughes Ridge and eventually into Smokemont Campground. Hike this section slowly and admire the enormous old hemlocks and yellow buckeyes.

A few years ago we walked upstream along the south fork of the Merced River, within the boundaries of Yosemite. We were reminded of that experience when we sat looking at Raven Fork, though the lushness of the rhododendron, the mossy rocks, and the giant trees gave this setting an unmistakable eastern appearance. The power, the deep pools of water, and the massive rocks strewn haphazardly along the streambed had a similar appearance to the Merced. From a sturdy iron bridge you can look down into the clear water, or you can wade or swim from the boulders beneath the bridge. Across the bridge is a small, boulder-sheltered campsite (# 47).

Lovers of wilderness and trout fishermen speak of the upper reaches of the Raven Fork with true regard. It is known for its clear, swift, cascading water, running through huge boulders set deep within a canyonlike, mountain-sided valley. It is said to be one of the most beautiful, as well as unspoiled, areas within the park.

In former times an unmaintained manway descended from McGee Springs into the Big Pool of the Raven Fork. The pool is said to be particularly lovely, but the hike is strenuous and hazardous. Our curiosity was excited because of the primitive qualities ascribed to the Raven Fork area, and we took the easier walk there. We stopped just beyond the bridge by which the Enloe Creek Trail crosses the Raven Fork. Big Pool is several miles upstream of here with no trail to follow.

If you go, we suggest you take a camera. You will find pretty little shimmers of water descending over flat rocks and an amazing assortment of fungi, mosses, and ferns. You will see big rocks, overhangs, and a glimpse of things that lure trout fishermen into the mountains.

Other Walks
(Ask the Park Service for details.)

Hughes Ridge Trail is a 5.2-mile foot and horse trail to the Appalachian Trail. It can be reached from Chasteen Creek Trail from Smokemont or from Enloe Creek Trail (See Walk 31). There are excellent spring and summer wildflowers.

Newton Bald Trail starts on the Newfound Gap Road opposite the Smokemont Campground turnoff. It climbs 2,900 feet to the Newton Bald on the Thomas Divide in 5 miles. You need not go to the top for a good view. There is one at 3.8 miles on a lesser ridge. The once-grassy bald is now a second-growth forest.

The first 2.5 miles of **Chasteen Creek Trail** is a service road that forks off to the right from the Bradley Fork Trail. (See the Smokemont Loop, Walk 29.) It climbs all the way up to Hughes Ridge and has several good views along the way. There is a turn-around at the end of the service road. The trail continuing from here is a horse trail.

Tree on Stilts

Bryson City Area

32. Deep Creek Loop
33. Beaugard Ridge–Noland Divide Trail
34. Noland Creek
Other Walks: Thomas Divide Trail, Lakeshore Trail–Gold Mine
Loop, Forney Creek–Bear Creek Trail–Jumpup Ridge

32. DEEP CREEK LOOP

Distance: 4 miles

Difficulty: Easy to moderate

Elevation: Trail is fairly level for 1.5 miles, then climbs over a ridge 420 feet (1,980 feet to 2,400 feet) in 0.5 mile, drops down again and returns along a barely perceptible grade.

How to get there: Trail begins at a gate near the parking area at the end of the Deep Creek Road, which continues another half mile beyond the bridge leading to the campground. The trail sign indicates the way to the Indian Creek Trail.

As you walk up Deep Creek, you walk into Horace Kephart territory. "When I first came into the Smokies the whole region was one of superb forest primeval," Kephart wrote in 1925 to describe the forest he had known twenty years earlier. "I lived for several years in the heart of it . . . it was always clear and fragrant, always vital, growing new shapes of beauty from day to day." Maybe you've read Kephart's *Camping and Woodcraft* and *Our Southern Highlanders*—each with a special charm to recommend it.

This downstream stretch along Deep Creek was Horace Kephart's favorite camping ground. A plaque was erected in 1931 at the Bryson place in his honor by a Boy Scout troop, also named after him, in Bryson City. Today his old friends in the watershed are gone, but some of the old trees are still standing. There were a number of narrow bridges to cross when he went up to his camp. Now the trail is wide, the bridges are fewer and more substantial, and a horse-use campsite occupies the old grounds. The distance is 12 miles in and out, so we do not suggest you go the whole way. For a pleasant day walk follow the road as it climbs about 50 feet and levels off. Deep Creek will be on your right. Within 200 yards or so the Toms Branch Falls spill down into the stream from the opposite bank. At 0.5 mile a bridge carries you to the east bank and continues to a fork in the road at 0.8 mile. Here, take the right fork, the Indian Creek Trail. A short distance along it you will see the Indian Creek Falls below you on your left.

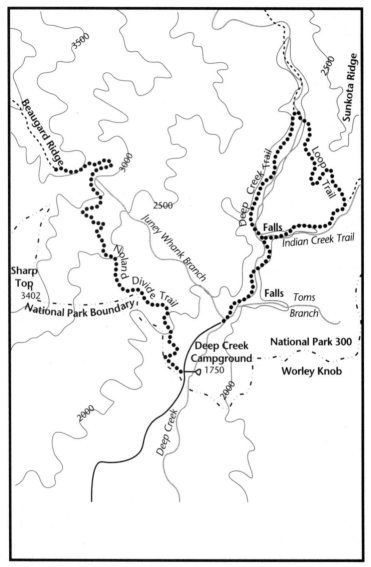

Deep Creek Loop and Beaugard Ridge–Noland Divide Trail

Continue along this trail and look for Loop Trail branching out to the left, well marked, at 1.5 miles. Follow this trail, leading back to Deep Creek. This connecting trail is 1 mile long and requires a 420-foot climb up over the lower portion of the Sunkota Ridge. You will be able to judge your progress since you can easily make out the crestline against the sky. Stop and rest as you gain on it. At the crest, Sunkota Ridge Trail goes right and meets Thomas Divide Trail in 8.6 miles. Going down will be easy—a nice grade. Then you cross over to the west side of Deep Creek on the bridge to return 0.5 mile before crossing again to the east bank. You are now back at the 1-mile junction. From here back to the gate you will be retracing your steps. Many people swim or ride inner tubes (which can be rented just outside the park); you can also find a quiet place to sit on a boulder and soak your feet.

33. BEAUGARD RIDGE–NOLAND DIVIDE TRAIL

Distance: 5 miles (up and back)
Difficulty: Moderate
Elevation: Vertical rise is 1,820 feet in 2.5 miles (1,780 feet to 3,600 feet). Trail presents a steady, graded climb. Return trip is easy.
How to get there: Trail begins to the left of the bridge at the entrance to the Deep Creek Campground. You will find the NOLAND DIVIDE TRAIL sign pointing the direction.

Each walk has a certain individuality, although it is not always easy to delineate. The Beaugard Ridgetop has a secret solemnity. There are great views to the south over Deep Creek Valley. To the east you can see the Blue Ridge Parkway. The lookout opening, the goal of the walk, is about 1,800 feet above Deep Creek Campground. There are other, lesser openings after the first half mile, which also have nice views. If you wish to extend your walk beyond the big lookout, there is a narrow gap a mile beyond with still another fine view east and west.

The path is well graded. Nowhere is the slope terribly steep. The footing is exceptionally good and it is very easy coming down. It starts off working westward and upward until you have gone about three-quarters of a mile through dry pine forest. It then crests out on a lower knob and turns abruptly back toward the northeast. Here the path works its way up a graded ledge cut into the extremely steep eastern side of this higher ridge. The ledge winds considerably with the contours. You hop over the upper, very narrow stream of the Juney Whank Branch at about a mile and a half. (Below, on a short spur trail just before the Deep Creek Trail, Juney Whank Branch develops a beautiful waterfall.) There is another fine view southward at 2 miles. The trail "tops out" with a 180-degree turn a half mile later.

The walk begins in a level area but starts to climb in a half mile. It goes through pine woods, where the needles make comfortable walking. It then leads into dense, moist woods which were bright with deep blue spiderwort, blazing red firepink, and spiky white galax when we walked there in early summer. We were surprised to see the firepink in its prime in June. We had seen it in April and in May and expected that its blooming season was over. We are pleased to say wildflowers in the Smokies are where you find them.

We sat to have our sandwiches at the lookout just 2.5 miles along the trail. Gazing off at the serene mountains beyond, hearing the distant cry of the hawk, and smelling the pungent odors of the forest, we spoke of treasures simply not available at any auto pull-out overlook. The concept of eons of time is beyond the grasp of most of us. In a setting such as this, just looking at the movement in the sky makes you aware of the constant change to which the mountains have been subjected. You can appreciate more easily the timeless character here and the quality of the rich garden it has become today.

34. NOLAND CREEK

Distance: 6 miles (in and out)

Difficulty: Easy

Elevation: Vertical rise is 420 feet in 3 miles (1,800 feet to 2,220 feet). This is a service road, and seems level because of the gentle grade.

How to get there: Trail begins 7.1 miles from Bryson City just before the Noland Creek Bridge—a bridge high above the scenic trout stream below—on Lakeview Drive (known locally as the new Fontana Road). Park in a large pullout on the left and look for the trail sign just before the beginning of the bridge guardrail.

To gain access to walks in the southwestern section of the park, you go in through Bryson City. The nineteenth-century origins of its Swain County Courthouse are conspicuous, and it stands as a picturesque reminder of more gracious days. Wrought iron is common ornamentation in the town. Horace Kephart came here in 1904, and today a rock boulder marks his grave in the local cemetery. The town has a nice old-time atmosphere.

The Noland Creek Watershed is one of the two drainage areas that can be reached through Bryson City. There is a beautiful road called the Lakeview Drive that takes you there in 9 miles. Take the road north alongside the courthouse, cross the Tuckasegee River, and continue straight ahead. You drive along in nearly solitary splendor.

There is an overlook that will show you where you are in relation to Fontana Lake. Seven miles from the edge of town you will approach a bridge that curves with the contour of the road as it skirts the hill. Just before the bridge there is a parking lot to the left. Here you should leave your car. The trail is on the left side of the road between the parking lot and the bridge. You can walk 1 mile left to the lake's edge, but we turned right and went under the Noland Creek Bridge on the splendid, wide, former railroad right-of-way. This way you walk beside Noland Creek—an easy walk with few landmarks but a most pleasing ambience.

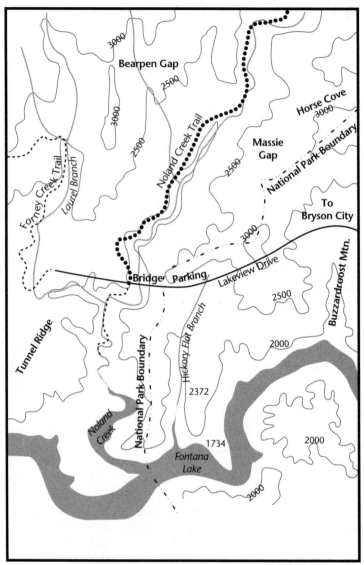

Noland Creek

Many pioneer families lived up Noland Creek in the olden times, including the clan of Noland. You will see various homestead sites and can recognize them from the cultivated red roses, daffodils, and forsythia now running rampant or the tall boxwoods that once announced the way to the front door. Hepatica, blood root, and early yellow violets now grow on the road bank and bloom in late March or April. Enjoy the beckoning sound and cooling sight of the creek as you go along. Look for a rill to your left which comes gushing down but is conducted under the road. Look also for a grove of white pine which varies the light and shade pattern of the hardwoods along the trail. At 3 miles there is a bridge across Noland Creek, which is a good place for lunch and a proper turnaround.

You may wish to go on to Solola Valley, which is up this road another mile or so. It is an old settlement where there is now a foundation of the old gristmill and a grove of walnut trees. From here on the Springhouse Branch Trail, which cuts off to the left from the Mill Creek Horse Camp, the trail reaches some of the original timber left in the upper reaches of this watershed. This land was farmland and never suffered the devastation of the loggers' axes to the extent of adjoining land where they practically leveled it. You may want to spare the effort and turn around at the bridge.

Other Walks

(Ask the Park Service for details.)

Thomas Divide Trail offers a ridge top walk from the Newfound Gap Road (see Walk 20) into the Deep Creek Campground. It is possible to walk the lower section from just beyond Indian Creek Falls (off Deep Creek Road—see Walk 20), reaching the ridge at Stone Pile Gap in about 1.5 miles.

Lakeshore Trail–Gold Mine Loop goes through the 375 yard "Tunnel to Nowhere," built and abandoned in the 1960s, and then loops toward Fontana Lake past old homesites. It starts at the end of Lakeview Road.

Forney Creek–Bear Creek Trail–Jumpup Ridge. The Forney Creek Trail starts on the eastward end of Fontana Lake and runs 9 miles up the creek valley. You can reach the trail beginning from Lakeshore Trail at the end of Lakeview Road. Just a half mile along, the Bear Creek Trail veers off to the left. It is an old road that climbs to the top of Jumpup Ridge, 3,300 feet, in 3.5 miles. (Elevation at the start of the trail is 1,710 feet.)

Fontana Lake Area

35. Hazel Creek
36. Shuckstack–Appalachian Trail
Other Walks: Eagle Creek Trail, Twentymile Creek Trail, Lakeshore Trail

White Azaleas, Gregory Bald

35. HAZEL CREEK

Distance: 6.6 miles (in and out)
Difficulty: Easy
Elevation: Vertical rise is 258 feet in 3.3 miles (1,742 feet to 2,000 feet). (It seems level all the way.)
How to get there: Trail begins at the marina at Fontana Village.

As you drive the road (N.C. 28) that parallels the southern border of the park, look across Fontana Lake to the wooded mountains that rise steeply along the far shore. You might imagine this part of the park would be quite impenetrable. And so it is, except for those who enjoy a short boat trip as a prelude to a pleasant walk.

For a modest sum the marina at Fontana Village will shuttle hikers across Fontana Dam. Call Fontana Village Marina (828-498-2211, ext. 227) for information and reservations. Small boat rental may be possible, but only for experienced boaters. It is a thirty-minute ride across the lake and up a finger of water that was once the deep valley drained by the creek. You can fancy that you're traveling on one of the Alpine lakes of northern Italy. The mountains literally rear out of the water and the trees march down to its edges. Nowhere is there a habitation. Your only company will be the birds and an occasional angler. Look for a heron to flutter away as you come in close to shore.

There is an informal landing at the mouth of the creek. A boat or two may already be here, because this is a favorite haunt of fishermen.

You start out on a well-kept road and pass a back-country campsite (#86) in a few hundred yards where the road makes its first crossing of the creek. You are then in what was once the village of Proctor, a thriving lumber community of one thousand souls, several stores, schools, and churches, and a movie theater. One house used by a summer ranger and his family remains. Rose bushes and flowers grow where other houses and gardens once stood. On the left of this pleasant path you'll see a depression that

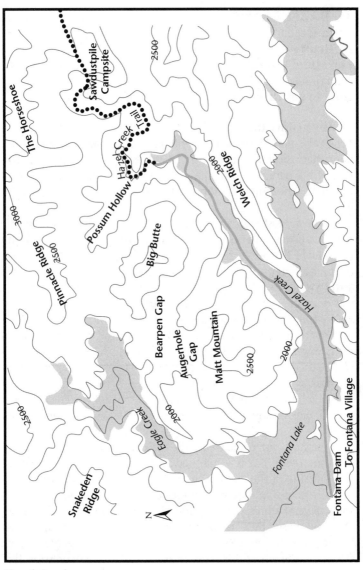

Hazel Creek

was once a millpond, the remains of a pump station that used to pump the creek water into the pond when needed, and the tumbled chimney of an old drying kiln. These were part of a commercial lumberyard that produced and shipped finished lumber until 1928.

This sandy walkway is generally wide and nice underfoot as it travels along the stream. There are ways to go out onto the water's edge. It is an interesting creek with runs and rills and trout pools and little tumbling falls. It is lined with laurel and azalea. The white azalea here is famous and easily located by its fragrance. Laurel was in bloom when we were here in June, with rosettes looking like perfect peonies. Reintroduced river otters have been seen from some of the creek bridges.

We made our objective the Sawdustpile (#85), the second backcountry campsite at 3.3 miles. We spread out our sandwiches on a rock and enjoyed the sun. After a lazy spell we walked on to the nearby fishermen's "Brown Pool" in the creek. After admiring it, we turned around and made our way back to the boat landing.

36. SHUCKSTACK–APPALACHIAN TRAIL

Distance: 7 miles (up and back)
Difficulty: Strenuous
Elevation: Vertical rise is 2,120 feet in 4.5 miles (1,900 feet to 4,020 feet). The Appalachian Trail to the lookout is steadily upward. By comparison the return will be easy.
How to get there: Trail begins 0.6 mile beyond Fontana Dam. Drive across the dam and take a right at the fork of the paved road, or you might choose to walk across the scenic dam and add an extra mile each way.

From the southwest the Appalachian Trail enters the Great Smoky Mountains National Park at Fontana Dam, the highest dam (480 feet) east of the Rocky Mountains. It is certainly impressive as its looming bulk holds back the Little Tennessee River and forms a

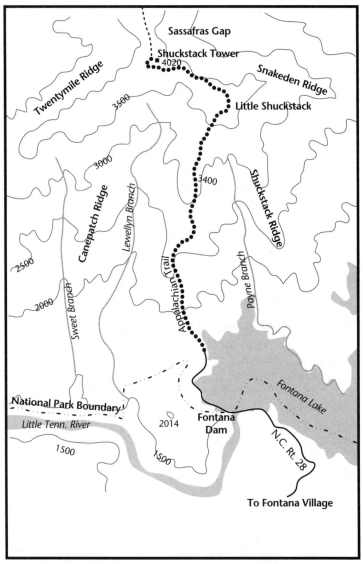

Shuckstack–Appalachian Trail

large lake in the midst of forest and mountains. You must cross the dam and then go a half mile ahead on the paved road to where the trail begins. It will be on your left and rises 2,100 feet in the 3.5 miles from there to the tower. You can see the tower as you cross the dam. To reach it is an achiever's walk.

The path rises quite gently at first. It is well graded with switchbacks. Every time the pushing upward begins to pall, there is a compensating level area to get your wind back. This walk is worthwhile only if you plan to go at least 3 miles on it, where it breaks into the open on a rocky ledge with fine southward views. By that time you will want to go on the extra half mile to the tower.

At about 2 miles out, the trail arcs to the left after a sharp right-hand turn. You can look up and see the top of Shuckstack. This is a moment of encouragement, for here the peak does not look so far away.

As we emerged from the woods, the feeling was that of a lazy summer's day, although May was not yet over. The grass had grown up and had gone to seed. Insects droned and the sky had just a few fleecy clouds. The wildflowers were in splendid array. The saxifrage was tall and willowy in the cracks of the rock face, where water seeped out and supported moss and lichen gardens below. Columbine and Indian paintbrush were brilliant in the sun. This is the spot for refreshment on the way up, with the ridges of the Nantahala and Snowbird mountains spread out before you.

Having regained your strength, the last, quite steep climb to the junction with the side trail that takes you up to the tower does not seem the half mile that it is. The elevation here is 4,020 feet. Winter views in every direction are unlimited, while in summer, the views are somewhat obscured by fast-growing trees, though glimpses of the surrounding mountains are still impressive.

Other Walks
(Ask the Park Service for details.)

Eagle Creek Trail starts on Fontana Lake, but at the western end. Getting to this trailhead requires a boat shuttle, just as in

Walk 35. Cross Fontana Lake to near the point where Eagle Creek enters the lake. This is a shorter crossing than to Hazel Creek. The trail extends along the creek, which is popular with fishermen, for almost 9 miles. One mile up this trail the **Lakeshore Trail** continues eastwardly on an overgrown old road along the Pinnacle Creek. To reach its trailhead, it is necessary to cross Eagle Creek on a footbridge.

Twentymile Creek Trail is an old service road from the ranger station on Route 28 up to Shuckstack in 5.3 miles. Many backpackers seem to prefer it because it is not as steep as the Shuckstack–Appalachian Trail.

Lakeshore Trail. Just beyond the Shuckstack trailhead is the Lakeshore Trail sign, showing 5.5 miles to Lost Cove Trail and 6.5 miles to Eagle Creek Trail. It's a good path for stretching the legs, but is neither wide nor graded except for the two road segments, one at the trailhead and another about 1.3 miles beyond.

Balsams Area

37. Flat Creek Trail
38. Balsam High Top
Other Walks: Rough Fork Trail, Cataloochee Divide Trail, Palmer Creek Trail

Black Bear Cub

37. FLAT CREEK TRAIL

Distance: 4.5 miles (over and back)
Difficulty: Easy
Elevation: In 2.25 miles the trail slides 520 feet (5,320 feet to 4,800 feet). Return is well graded and hardly a climb.
How to get there: Trail begins at the parking area for the Heintooga Picnic Area. You will find this at the end of the spur road off the Blue Ridge Parkway.

The trail starts just beyond the Heintooga Overlook. You can park your car there. Enjoy the view before proceeding. The view is a dramatic beginning—grand and impersonal, whereas the Flat Creek Trail is a highly intimate walk. Just past a trailside drinking fountain, take the right fork down into shady spruce woods.

Flat Creek is a high mountain brook that keeps the area immediately around it damp enough to support grass, trees of both modest and immense size, and a showcase of ferns and mosses. The trail is not a long one. We went out just over 2 miles to another lovely view—not the equal of Heintooga, but satisfying. It goes through beech, birch, and oak woods, splashed throughout with Fraser fir. It hardly inclines or declines at all. It is soft underfoot and often has open places, including a couple of heath balds with lush laurel and blackberry bushes that should be weighted to the ground in July. When we walked in mid-June it was between seasons for wildflowers, but buds of fly poison, tassel rue, and false hellebore could be found.

The shades of green on the Flat Creek Trail in June go from the deep dark of the balsam through the shiny forest green of the sedges and to the apple green or chartreuse of the newly unfolded ferns. The shades in between are innumerable. And all textures are represented, from the fine soft sphagnum moss to the coarse shoots of the sedge. The effect is that of a beautifully designed tapestry executed entirely in shades of green. You are likely to find a spot for lunch here in the sun on a log surrounded by tall laurel bushes covered in showers of pink blossoms.

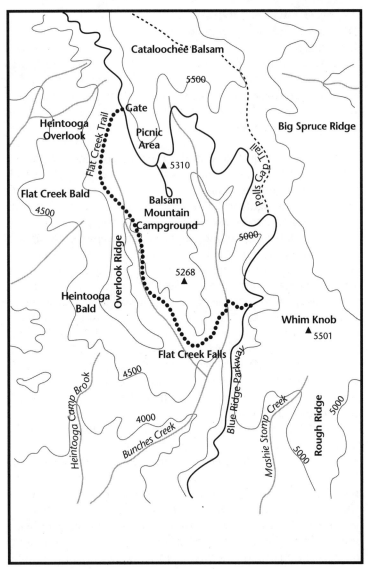

Flat Creek Trail

At about 1.75 miles a path goes off to the right to Flat Creek Falls. If you follow it down, the footing becomes difficult as it nears the roar of the falls. The path forks; left is a very rough path (avoid in wet weather) to the bottom of the two-tiered falls. The right fork goes to the top of the falls. In low water you can rock-hop across and find a slightly better scramble to the bottom on the other side. After a side trip to the falls, you can continue on Flat Creek Trail out onto the ridge ahead for a surprisingly lovely view to the southwest.

To sum it up: You walk down this trail (not much of a drop—100 feet or so), a gradual slope down through a spruce-fir woods, grassy on the ground; along a creeklet (not nearly a full creek-size stream); out on two or three enclosed meadows (warm and sunny in good weather). At about 2 miles, come to good views toward south and west through small openings in the trees. It is quiet, subtle, and enchanting. You may want to bring a camera in case you come across a purple-fringed orchid in bloom.

You can return to Heintooga Overlook and your car at this point, or you can continue another 0.5 mile to Heintooga Road near Polls (Pauls on the road sign) Gap.

38. BALSAM HIGH TOP

Distance: 7 miles (up and back)
Difficulty: Moderate
Elevation: Vertical rise is 1,217 feet in 3.5 miles (4,423 feet to 5,640 feet). Trail presents a steady, gradual climb and an easy return.
How to get there: Trail begins on the one-way Balsam Mountain Road (closed in winter) 8.5 miles from the Heintooga Picnic Area. It is a marked gated service road on your right.

This is a backwoods walk. It can give you a feeling of being miles away in perfect solitude. Entirely in the higher elevations, it quickly gets into the spruce-fir forest. Thick grass along the trail

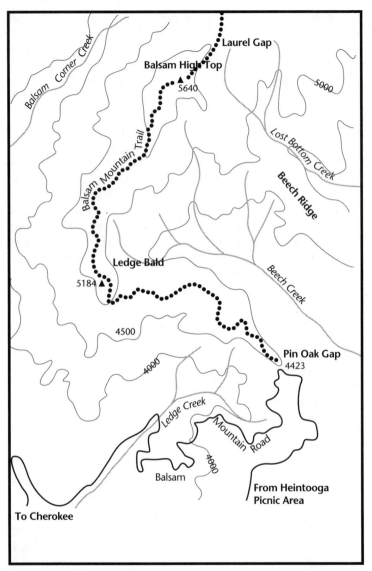

Balsam High Top

and in open areas is the only reminder of livestock grazing here until 1936, when most of this ridge was grassy bald.

To reach Pin Oak Gap, the starting point of this trail, you have to drive almost 9 miles down the one-way dirt Round Bottom Road from the Heintooga Picnic Area. You then must continue 21 more miles to reach the Newfound Gap Road near Cherokee. By itself this route is a fine forest experience. In early morning the light is soft, and the air is clear. Drive slowly and you may be lucky enough to catch sight of a ruffed grouse escorting a brood across the road.

The trail has an excellent underfooting. Although it was a service road, it does not appear to have heavy use now. It follows the spine of the ridge, climbing rather steeply. It then levels off, drops, and climbs to level off again. It repeats this rippling ascent without switchbacks, only curving and winding along easily. You are aware that you are on a ridge because it is open as you look out to either side, and there is the light of the sky in a band and the smoky blur of the next ridge in a darker band below.

This path has no rough spots or streams to cross and recross. But on any walk there are always small surprises. The day we walked here we came upon a grouse in the path. Luckily she did not see us as we stopped short at the turn. She was checking out the path to make sure it was safe for her brood to cross. In June, flame azalea, mountain laurel, fire pink, and pink lady's-slipper bloom along the trail.

There is no best time to walk this trail, but if you go on a reasonably clear day, you will be rewarded with a beautiful view of Spruce Mountain and the Cataloochee Basin. Each season has its own beauty. If you go in the spring, summer, or fall, you may be inspired to think of the scenery as it appears in the winter. As you come down off the hills, look around and try to imagine these ridges in a light snow when the oaks and maples have lost their leaves, when vistas are more open, and when the wind has more force.

131

Other Walks

(Ask the Park Service for details.)

On the Blue Ridge Parkway Spur, from Polls Gap:

Rough Fork Trail will take you out on an old railroad grade along the Big Fork Ridge. It goes 2.6 miles above 4,600 feet before dropping down into Cataloochee Valley.

Cataloochee Divide Trail follows an old railroad grade along the park boundary and along the ridge of the divide.

From Round Bottom Road (one-way) out of Heintooga Picnic Area:

Palmer Creek Trail starts about 2 miles farther on, but before the Balsam Mountain Trail. If you follow it 3 miles, it takes you down 1,520 feet to the Pretty Hollow Creek in Cataloochee.

Cataloochee–Big Creek Area

39. Big Creek
40. Davenport Gap–Appalachian Trail
41. Rough Fork Trail
42. Caldwell Fork–Boogerman Trail Loop
Other Walks: Cataloochee Divide Trail, Little Cataloochee Trail,
Mount Sterling Fire Tower, Pretty Hollow Creek Trail

Directions to Big Creek from Interstate 40: Take exit 451 (Waterville Road), which you will find just about on the North Carolina–Tennessee border. Drop down beside the highway and turn right to cross the Pigeon River on the bridge. Continue 2 miles to an intersection. Straight ahead, past the Waterville power plant and Mountain Mama's country store, is the park boundary, the ranger station, and the Big Creek Primitive Campground. To your right the road leads in 1 mile to Davenport Gap. It is possible to drive on to Cataloochee from this intersection by continuing left beyond Mount Sterling. This road is unpaved, narrow, and quite curvy.

Directions to Cataloochee from Interstate 40: Take exit 20 (N.C. 276, Maggive Valley), go right and turn right immediately onto Cove Creek Road. Enter park after about 3 miles.

Water Slide

39. BIG CREEK

Distance: 4 miles (in and out)

Difficulty: Easy

Elevation: Vertical rise represents 580 feet in 2 miles (1,700 feet to 2,240 feet). Trail is well graded and an easy return. Walk can easily be extended.

How to get there: Trail begins at Big Creek Primitive Campground, which is a half mile beyond the ranger station. You'll find ample parking there. The trail goes off to the right above the campground.

The Big Creek section used to be one of the more remote in the Smoky Park until I–40 came along with an exit not very far from it. The drive into the Big Creek Primitive Campground is a lovely one. The trail is a graded service road running along Big Creek. Once it was a railroad right-of-way. If you were to follow it about 6 miles, you would find a junction with several of the ridge trails. There are, consequently, all kinds of walkers on this trail—those going to higher elevations, fishermen, photographers, and campers out for a stroll.

This walk goes through a fine hardwood forest, grown back substantially since logging was stopped there. At first the road, which starts at what was the old logging camp, rises above the water. Its ascent is very gradual. At 1 mile it passes some very large and imposing rocks. One formation, up the steep slope on the right, suggests a huge room and was used as such in logging days before workers got their own lodgings. It is worth a scramble up the faint trail. Then along about 1.5 miles, with the creek now only a little below the road, there is a most magnificent deepening in it, appropriately called "midnight hole." It is landscaped by gigantic gray boulders, and it is a deep blue and exceedingly clear. Trout are visible scooting around. A quick swim here will cool you off on the hottest summer day.

At 2 miles Mouse Creek Falls tumbles into Big Creek from the far bank, but you must walk behind the hitching rails for horses for a good view. This is a good turnaround point if you want only a short walk.

If you keep onward, in .25 mile the road crosses the creek on a

135

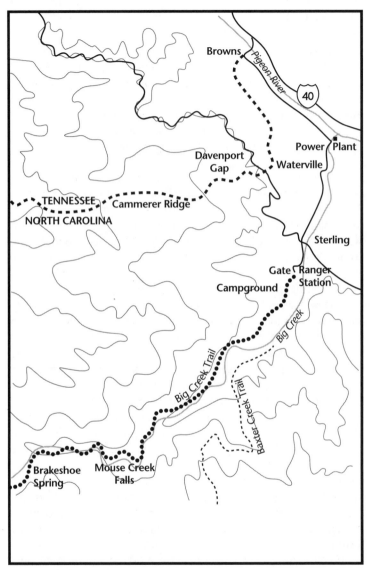

Big Creek

bridge. The pools below harbor the silhouettes of trout. At 2.9 miles there is another logical stopping place, the Brakeshoe Spring. Here a thirsty railroad engineer used to stop for a drink as his train went up and down the mountain. To make drinking from the spring easier, he drove a brakeshoe into the source. This provided a convenient conduit for the water. To recognize the spring, look for a spot where water flows across the trail from rock face on the left. The brakeshoe was driven into the largest trickle down the rock face. However, it rusted and slipped out a few years ago.

The boulders in front of Brakeshoe Spring serve as a good picnic area. You can enjoy your lunch in some of the especially beautiful surroundings the forests provide. Take every scrap or wrapping with you when you are finished. It is essential we follow the rules and never litter. While it may seem unnecessary to make this plea, if you talk with maintenance staff, you would believe how careless many visitors are!

40. DAVENPORT GAP–APPALACHIAN TRAIL

Distance: 9 miles (in and out)
Difficulty: Moderate to strenuous
Elevation: Vertical rise represents 1,800 feet in 4.5 miles (1,700 feet to 3,500 feet). Trail is well graded and an easy return.
How to get there: Although the Appalachian Trail crosses Route 32 at Davenport Gap, it is best to park below at the Big Creek Ranger Station. Parking is a problem at Davenport Gap. Because it is so isolated, cars parked here have frequently been broken into, and the Park Service advises against it. This makes a 1.5-mile walk to the trailhead.

The Appalachian Trail is well marked. When it crosses Route 32 you step directly onto it. This section is very beautiful, although there are no outstanding views. It takes off uphill on an old service road. The distance from Davenport Gap to the large Appalachian Trail shelter (remodeled in 1998) is a steady climb of almost a mile. The road then comes to a halt, and the trail continues veering left

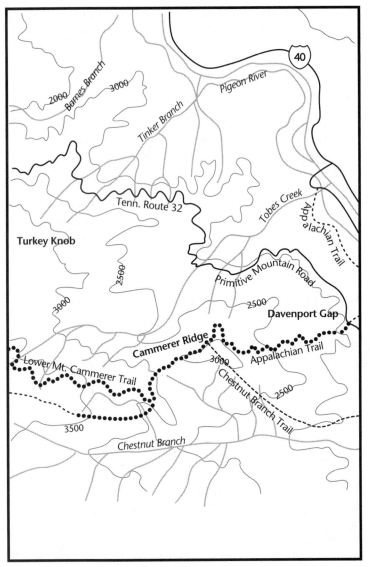

Davenport Gap–Appalachian Trail

through mazes of dwarf iris and fern. The trail climbs for another 1.25 miles and then levels off. It enters a rhododendron grove and goes along level for a pleasant half mile, where you can retrieve your breath and straighten out your knees.

At 1.9 miles there is a National Park Service sign on the left for Chestnut Branch Trail to Big Creek. Wait for a good day for this walk if you can. Many Smokies walks are actually enhanced by showery weather or at least not spoiled by it. This one seemed different to us. It was not quiet and mysterious with old trees and watery cascades. It was more open and younger, wanting the illumination of the sun.

In another mile, where the Appalachian Trail begins its 1,500-foot ascent to the Mount Cammerer Tower, a trail branches off to the right for Cosby Campground. The Mount Cammerer Fire Tower is the usual goal, but there is no use to spoil a day's outing by feeling you must press on. That would be a 14-mile trip and a climb of over 3,275 feet. We chose to stroll along the Lower Mount Cammerer Trail. This trail leads toward Cosby, a nice level path following the contour of the slope, crossing some sweetwater springs and lined with flowers. It allows a leisurely, breath-catching walk and a feeling of isolation. Moving along the steep side of Mount Cammerer, you feel that you are walking very near the sky. We listened to the involved mating song of the grosbeak and watched them diving about among April's mountain silverbell blossoms. We then turned and retraced our steps.

41. ROUGH FORK TRAIL

Distance: 2 miles (in and out)
Difficulty: Easy
Elevation: Trail is virtually level, 2,750 feet to 2,886 feet in 1 mile and can easily be extended into a longer walk.
How to get there: Trail begins at the very end of the Cataloochee Valley Road.

The Cataloochee section of the park is very secluded—a high valley that would be called "a hemmed-in hollow" in the Ozarks.

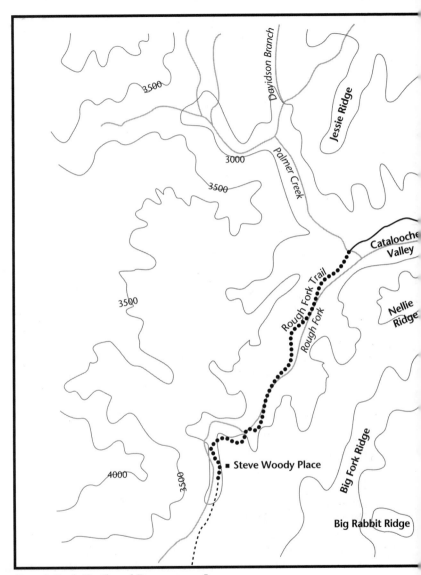

Rough Fork Trail and Boogerman Loop

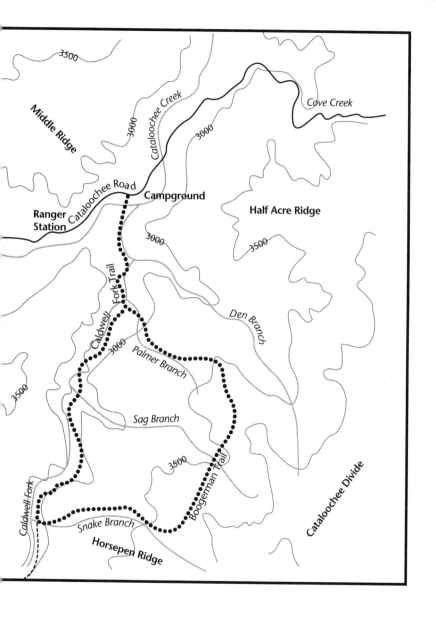

It is a narrow valley—not spacious like Cades Cove. The fields are beautiful with a kind of hay that looks lavender in the sun. It is more contained, and more intimate, and runs the length of Rough Fork, a sylvan brook.

To get to Cataloochee requires driving over the mountains on unpaved, very winding mountain roads. (Ask the ranger of the Oconaluftee Visitor Center for directions.) The roads are well kept and used, but one must drive slowly and carefully. Once you reach the valley, there is a hardtop road for nearly the length of it. Cataloochee has a very special quality, but this could change quickly with overcrowding. Its trails all permit horseback riding, and when the water is high, there is inevitably roiled-up mud from the horse hoofs. You will not find it a problem if you wear thick-soled boots.

The Rough Fork Trail starts at the very end of the road through the Cataloochee Valley. You will see some of the old houses, a church, and a school and savor the secret charm of the place at once. When you can drive no further, park. The trail is a continuation of the road, running alongside the Rough Fork creekbed on quite level ground.

For an easy walk and an outing anyone can make, follow the trail for 1 mile. Cross the stream three times on foot bridges and break into a clearing. The ambience of the woods through which the trail runs is splendid—sylvan and cool. In the clearing is Steve Woody's place, an old cabin now faced with white clapboard. You can wander through the two-story cabin and imagine living there between the apple orchard and the creek.

If you would like to explore further, you can continue on the trail. It runs up from here to the ridge of the Balsam Mountains (along which the spur road off the Blue Ridge Parkway leads to the Heintooga Picnic Area). It gains almost 3,000 feet in elevation. Undaunted, we walked another mile or two. In a half mile you have to ford a shallow stream where there is a back-country campsite (#40). From there the trail begins its climb. On the slope, big trees, especially yellow poplar, maple, and oak, begin to appear. You may want to turn around at this point.

42. CALDWELL FORK–BOOGERMAN TRAIL LOOP

Distance: 7.4 miles

Difficulty: Moderate

Elevation: Vertical rise represents 850 feet in just over 3 miles (2,750 feet to 3,500 feet). Trail is well graded. An easy return.

How to get there: Caldwell Fork Trail begins just beyond the Cataloochee Campground, crossing the Rough Fork on a log bridge to your left.

This is the kind of undemanding walk where you can look carefully around and enjoy all you see, hear, and smell. A profusion of the most splendid flowers in the park grows here, along with fine stands of hemlock, oak, poplar, and maple. The forest floor is strewn with fallen chestnut trees. The road you will walk and the property it goes through belonged to Robert Palmer, a shy recluse who lived in a cabin he built high on a hill above Cataloochee Valley to get away from people. His neighbors called him the Boogerman. He knew a beautiful, secluded site when he saw one and would never allow his timber to be cut.

It is easy to follow the path, but you must pay attention not to miss it. Starting is no problem, for just beyond the primitive campground, there is the longest foot bridge in the park, crossing the Rough Fork. It is on your left and marked the Caldwell Fork Trail, a well-used horse trail. Take this trail .75 mile (counting this first bridge) to the second log bridge. The Boogerman Trail, closed to horses, leaves the main trail just 25 paces on your left beyond this bridge and can easily be overlooked.

The trail then climbs about 800 feet on lovely, springy pine needles. It leads around the side of a hill with peek-through views into Cataloochee Valley. It levels off and turns abruptly to the right. It then passes the scarce remnants of an old split-rail fence on your right and reaches a clearing. The trail will cross over a tiny stream on a small plank bridge, and just ahead you will find the first trickle of water. It was in this general area that the Boogerman had his cabin. If you wish to shorten the walk, this is a good turnaround, making the total distance less than 4 miles.

Just beyond the field and past the little brook we found in early summer a lily-leafed twayblade and many purple-fringed orchids. The rattlesnake plantain orchid was getting ready to bloom, and the standout color was the yellow of the evening primrose that bloomed in profusion along the way.

As you continue, the trail climbs another 100 feet before starting back down to the Caldwell Fork. Nearing this junction you will come to some chestnut logs, the remains of Carson Messer's log cabin, and several moss-covered, stone walls such as those associated with New England. When the path rejoins the Caldwell Fork Trail, you are 2.5 miles from the start. Turn right here. The path, both rocky and muddy at times, crosses and recrosses the brook. Hikers can use excellent foot bridges; horses have to wade across the rocky creek. Look for bleeding heart, pink lady's-slipper, and many other flowers along the trail bank.

Other Walks
(Ask the Park Service for details.)

From the Cove Creek Gap, as you come into Cataloochee:

Cataloochee Divide Trail runs southwesterly along the park boundary, ending at Polls Gap on the Blue Ridge Parkway Spur.

Off Old North Carolina Route 284 (now N.C. 1397):

Between Cove Creek Gap and Mount Sterling Gap the **Little Cataloochee Trail** leads along an old road into an area once rather heavily populated.

From Mount Sterling Gap climbing up to **Mount Sterling Fire Tower** is a 2,000-foot ascent in 2.5 miles. From here the views in all directions are great.

Starting at the Cataloochee Schoolhouse, in the valley:

Pretty Hollow Creek Trail leads into both the Pretty Hollow Creek and the Little Cataloochee trails.

Appendix I—Bird-Watching in Great Smoky Mountains National Park

~~~~~~~~~~~~~~~~~~~~~~~~~~~~~~~~~~

If you are even a casual bird watcher, you will understand how engrossed you can become after you have spotted your first warbler. You may regret the years you have taken your feathered friends for granted. Sorting out all these little flitting creatures, which come in many color combinations, and trying to bring song and bird together with nesting and migrating patterns can consume a lifetime. It is easy to get hooked, but do not let this pastime hinder your full enjoyment of the trail.

If you walk through the woods and are discouraged by not seeing any birds, perhaps you should know that birds are frightened by the slightest movement you make. Learn to become a statue! Take a lesson from the cat and learn the art of stalking. Watch to see a feather flash in the bushes, see it move, and follow it carefully. Some may fly away unidentified, but you will have success with a little perseverance.

Birds are creatures of habit. The Smokies have become permanent summer residences for eighty-seven species of them, and many migrants and strays appear here every year. However, you are most apt to see the ones that nest here.

Common birds found within the boundaries of Great Smoky Mountains National Park during the spring and summer months

Key:

A Abundant   F Fairly Common

C Common   U Uncommon

At Lower and Middle Elevations (more commonly)

Mourning Dove F
Yellow-billed Cuckoo F
Screech Owl F
Whip-poor-will F
Belted Kingfisher F
Eastern Phoebe C
Acadian Flycatcher C
Carolina Chickadee C
Carolina Wren C
Mockingbird U
Brown Thrasher F
Wood Thrush C
Eastern Bluebird F
Blue-gray Gnatcatcher C
Starling C
White-eyed Vireo F
Yellow-throated Vireo C
Red-eyed Vireo A
Black-and-white Warbler C
Worm-eating Warbler F

Golden-winged Warbler U
Yellow Warbler U
Black-throated Green Warbler F
Yellow-throated Warbler F
Prairie Warbler U
Ovenbird C
Louisiana Waterthrush C
Kentucky Warbler F
Yellow-breasted Chat U
Hooded Warbler C
American Redstart U
Common Grackle F
Summer Tanager U
Cardinal F
Indigo Bunting C
Chipping Sparrow C
Field Sparrow C
Song Sparrow C
American Goldfinch F

At Higher Elevations (more commonly)

Black-billed Cuckoo U
Black-capped Chickadee F
Red-breasted Nuthatch C
Tufted Titmouse C
Brown Creeper F
Winter Wren C
Veery C

Golden-crowned Kinglet C
Solitary Vireo C
Black-throated Blue Warbler C
Blackburnian Warbler F
Chestnut-sided Warbler C
Dark-eyed Junco (formerly
Slate-colored Junco) A

At All Elevations

Ruffed Grouse F

Chimney Swift C

Ruby-throated Hummingbird F

Yellow-shafted Flicker C

Pileated Woodpecker F

Hairy Woodpecker F

Downy Woodpecker F

Great Crested Flycatcher F

Eastern Wood Pewee C

Rough-winged Swallow F

Blue Jay C

Common Crow C

White-breasted Nuthatch F

Catbird F

Robin F

Cedar Waxwing F

Parula Warbler F

Yellowthroat F

Red Crossbill U

Rufous-sided Towhee F

Each of these seventy-two birds is listed by Arthur Stupka in his monumental study *Notes on the Birds of Great Smoky Mountains National Park* (University of Tennessee Press) as common or fairly common during the spring and summer months and hence is most likely to be seen by any observant visitor.

Stupka lists a total of 211 birds that have been positively identified here during the year. Although some, of course, have been migrants or rare transients, the majority have been observed with some frequency.

Among those birds who are *permanent residents, but uncommonly seen,* are:

Bobwhite

Turkey

Great Horned Owl

Barred Owl

Red-bellied Woodpecker

Red-headed Woodpecker

Yellow-bellied Sapsucker

Olive-sided Flycatcher

Common Raven

A field checklist of the birds of the Great Smoky Mountains is available from the National Park Service.

Appendix II—Information Resources

To receive more information about Great Smoky Mountains National Park, write to:

Great Smoky Mountains National Park
107 Park Headquarters Road
Gatlinburg, TN 37738

Or call the park at (423) 436–1200 for a daily recording of road and weather conditions and camping information

Call (423) 436–7318, ext. 22 and ask for a copy of *Smokies Guide*, the park newspaper, which features up-to-date information on interpretive programs and services. A great deal of information is also available on the official Great Smoky Mountains National Park Web site (http://www.nps.gov/grsm), which features an in-depth electronic visitor center and details on all aspects of the park.

You can self-register at many campsites within the park, but reservations are necessary at rationed sites and shelters. For more information on these sites and to make a reservation, call (423) 436–1231 between 8:00 A.M. and 6:00 P.M. daily.

Other Resources

Friends of the Great Smoky Mountains National Park
134 Court Avenue
Sevierville, TN 37862
(423) 436–2428

This organization helps the park through direct funding and by raising money for the park from outside sources.

Great Smoky Mountains Natural History Association
115 Park Headquarters Road
Gatlinburg, TN 37738
(423) 436–7318

The association can provide you with a catalog listing hiking guides, videos, maps, and other park information.

The Great Smoky Mountains Institute at Tremont
Education Program, Great Smoky Mountains National Park
107 Park Headquarters Road
Gatlinburg, TN 37738
(423) 448–6709

This center offers programs and workshops for all ages and groups. Programs range from slide shows and guided hikes to mountain music and wildlife exhibits. Week-long environmental education camps run through the school year, and summer camps, Elder Hostels, and Teacher workshops are scheduled in summer.

Smoky Mountain Field School
The University of Tennessee Community Programs
105 Conference Center Building
Knoxville, TN 37996–4110
(800) 284–8885

Offering hikes, outdoor adventures, and workshops on flora and fauna, this school operates in conjunction with the University of Tennessee.

The Appalachian Trail Conference
P.O. Box 236
Harpers Ferry, WV 25425

The ATC provides information about the entire Appalachian Trail, including the portion that passes through the Great Smokies.

National Park Rules and Regulations

- You must possess a back-country permit while camping in the back country (call 423–436–1231.)
- Camping is permitted only at designated sites and shelters.
- Use of rationed sites and shelters must be confirmed through the Backcountry Reservation Office.
- You may stay up to three consecutive nights at a site. You may not stay two nights in a row at a shelter.
- Maximum camping party size is eight.
- Open fires are prohibited except at designated sites. Use only wood that is dead and on the ground.
- Use of tents at shelters is prohibited.
- When food is not being consumed or transported, all food and trash must be suspended at least 10 feet off the ground and 4 feet from the nearest limb or trunk or shall be stored as otherwise designated.
- Toilet use must be at least 100 feet from a campsite water source and out of sight of the trail. Human feces must be buried in 6-inch-deep hole.
- All trash must be carried out.
- All plants, wildlife, and natural and historic features are protected by law. Do not cut, carve, or deface any trees or shrubs.
- Polluting park waters is prohibited; do not wash dishes or bathe with soap in a stream.
* Pets, motorized vehicles, and bicycles are not permitted in the back country.

- Firearms and hunting are prohibited.
- Feeding or harassing any wildlife is prohibited.

Visitor Centers

Sugarlands Visitor Center, near Gatlinburg, Tennessee
Oconaluftee Visitor Center, near Cherokee, North Carolina
Cades Cove Visitor Center, near Townsend, Tennessee

There are visitor centers outside the park in Gatlinburg, Townsend, and Knoxville, Tennessee, and in Franklin, North Carolina.

About the Authors

Rod and Priscilla Albright have always been avid walkers. They have made numerous expeditions into the state and national forests of the United States. They have walked the slopes of Kilimanjaro in Tanzania, the desert floors and canyons of Texas and Arizona, and the beaches off the Bay of Fundy. Their walking is not confined to the wilds. They also enjoy roaming the streets of London, Paris, and New York.

Their experience and enjoyment of the outdoors is reflected in their work. They have also written a book called *Short Nature Walks on Long Island*. Their membership in the Audubon Society, the Wilderness Society, and the Nature Conservancy is an indication of their ongoing interest and concern for the preservation of our natural resources.

About the Editor

Doris Gove is a biologist, a member of the Smoky Mountains Hiking Club, and a volunteer Appalachian Trail maintainer. She has written *Exploring the Appalachian Trail: Hikes in the Southern Appalachians* (Stackpole Books) and has contributed to *Hiking Trails of the Smokies* and *Discovering the Smokies: A Science Journal* (both published by the Great Smoky Mountains Natural History Association). She has also written four natural history books for children.